Prayers

for the

Road

Prayers
for the Road

PSALM MEDITATIONS FOR COLLEGE STUDENTS

THOMAS W. CURRIE III

Geneva Press
Louisville, Kentucky

Book design by Bonnie Campbell / Running Feet Books
Cover design © 2000 Pamela Poll Graphic Design, Colorado Springs, CO (719) 277-0052

First edition
Published by Geneva Press
Louisville, Kentucky

This book is printed on acid-free paper that meets the American National Standards Institute Z39.48 standard. ♾

PRINTED IN THE UNITED STATES OF AMERICA

00 01 02 03 04 05 06 07 08 09 — 10 9 8 7 6 5 4 3 2 1

Library of Congress Cataloging-in-Publication Data
Currie, Thomas W.
   Prayers for the road : Psalm meditations for college students / Thomas W. Currie III.
      p. cm.
   Includes bibliographical references.
   ISBN 0-664-50129-X (alk. paper)
      1. Bible. O.T. Psalms—Meditations. 2. College students—Religious life. 3. Christian life—Presbyterian authors. I. Title.

BV1430.4.C87 2000
242'.634—dc21   00-035370

In memory of my mother,
Anne Alison Dunklin Harrison Currie,
who taught me to pray
and
In honor of my father, Thomas W. Currie Jr.,
who sent me to college with a book of prayers

Introduction

This book of prayers, meditations, and readings is primarily for college students. In August 1998, a young woman in the church I pastor came to see me before she left to go off to college. She wanted to express her thanks for this congregation and for the life that had been mediated to her through this part of the body of Christ. She also wanted to voice her hopes and fears about the coming semester. In particular, she wanted to talk about her faith and the resources that might strengthen her for the days ahead. We spent some time talking about God and God's will for her life. At the end of that conversation, I wanted very much to give her something to take with her, and I realized I had nothing much to offer. So that day I began reflecting on these psalms and writing these prayers.

The young woman's name is Kristin Hedger, but these devotions are not for her alone. They are for any young person getting ready to go off to college. "Kristin," after all, is a Scandinavian variant on the name "Christian" and so these devotions are for any "Christian" who is looking for help along the road. Going to college may well be the "Christian's" first step away from home and toward that pilgrim's progress that is always beckoning. That progress has as its goal life with God, the God who always meets us along the way, and who, in Jesus Christ, promises to be God with us. Clearly this little book of prayers is not a road map or a comprehensive account of that journey. It is but a way to get started. My hope is that the young people of my own congregation and indeed in Christ's church everywhere will begin such a journey by reading a psalm each day and finding in the accompanying meditation and prayer the means for getting started on a life-time of following Jesus Christ.

Prayer is, among other things, hard work. It is a gift and a blessing, but it is also hard and sometimes humiliating work. And it is easy to grow discouraged along the way. It is important for those who begin such a journey to know that there are others ready to help them along the road, praying for them and with them even when they cannot pray for themselves. No one lives the Christian life alone. No one even prays alone. That is what it means to be part of the church: to acknowledge our need of others and to receive the gifts of their prayers and hopes. Underneath those gifts is an even larger one, the gift of Jesus Christ himself, who, Hebrews reminds us, prays for us and gives us confidence to draw near "to the throne of grace," and there to find "help in time of need." (Heb. 4:14–16) To pray is to acknowledge our need of him and to learn not to be embarrassed at such need but to find in his company that daring trust that is not afraid to ask.

It is radically counter to our usual expectations of students to think they might be interested in prayer. We have no trouble thinking that they are interested in drinking or partying or even studying, but praying seems a bit of a stretch. I wonder, though. Perhaps the time that young people are exploring many different options and taking up their own identities is just the time the church should be of help in calling to mind the way God shapes our core identity. That is what this book of prayers seeks to do: to encourage that practice of prayer and praise that the church has always cultivated as a means of being formed into Christ's own image. Here too we follow him, learning to pray with him, reading our lives in his light. If prayer is the means of digging out such a treasure, as John Calvin thought it was, then we would do well to get used to the shovel that has been placed in our hands and become practiced in its use. In any case, I hope this book of psalms and meditations and prayers serves as such a shovel, a hand tool that can be used to start the digging. And when this tool wears out, the students who have started here will be able to find better tools elsewhere and wiser craftspeople to guide and direct them.

I have had a good deal of help in preparing these devotional readings. I would like to thank my former secretary, Nancy Wilbourn, for her patient and thorough reading of an earlier manuscript. She corrected many flaws and saved me from numerous errors and did it all with the grace she regularly shares with those who depend on her for guidance and help. The errors that remain are, of course, my own responsibility.

I would also like to thank Heather Mauzé, director of Ministry for Youth and Children in this congregation, who made many valuable suggestions, nearly all of which I have adopted. In addition, I would like to thank Bill Wilson, the moderator of the 197th General Assembly, and his wife, Marion, who encouraged me to think that this book might be worthy of publication. Similarly, I want to thank my friend, Robert Bullock Jr., editor of *The Presbyterian Outlook,* for his encouragement and help. Finally, I want to thank the session and congregation of First Presbyterian Church, Kerrville, for their patience during the writing and revising of this manuscript. I have been particularly blessed with a group of dedicated folk, led by Maud Jennings, who read this manuscript and made many valuable suggestions. They include Chris and Del Davis, Tom Stoner, Bertha Priour, Yvonne Miller, Marcia Smith, Leah Martin, and Louise Larson.

The readings included in this book are taken from the New Revised Standard Version of the Bible. However, we live in an age when there are many excellent translations and not a few helpful paraphrases. If the student who uses these devotionals wishes to make use of another translation or paraphrase, so much the better.

INTRODUCTION

In one of her essays, Flannery O'Connor quoted Saint Cyril of Jerusalem as saying: "The dragon sits by the side of the road, watching those who pass. Beware lest he devour you. We go to the Father of souls, but it is necessary to pass by the dragon."[1] We do not like to think that there are dragons in the world, much less that we must walk past them. But those who follow Jesus Christ learn very quickly that dragons do exist and to walk by them requires that we have a "weapon of the Spirit." Prayer is such a weapon. Rather than being a retreat to which we repair in the face of a difficult world, it is more often a way of engaging the dragon in his own cave. But just there do we discover that we are not alone but are in the company of a Lamb who defeats every dragon and who refuses to let us be separated from his love or be denied his victory. This Lamb has gathered about him "myriads of myriads and thousands of thousands," and they sing with a full voice, "Worthy is the Lamb that was slaughtered, to receive power and wealth and wisdom and might and honor and glory and blessing!" (Rev. 5:11–12) To pray in a world beset with dragons is to learn the song of this Lamb and to trust in his victory. That is how dragons are faced down and how Christians find the courage along the road.

CHRIST THE KING SUNDAY 1998

---

1. Flannery O'Connor, "The Fiction Writer and His Country," in *Mystery and Manners* (New York: Noonday Press, 1969), 35.

Foreword

Dear Kristin:

You came by the church today, and we talked in my study for a long time. You told me that you were getting ready to leave for college, and you wanted to come by and see your pastor before you left. I did not tell you then what a great honor you did me in coming by, but you made me feel very proud to be your pastor.

I wanted to give you a present, a book, something not only to remember me by, but something of use to you in the days ahead. I didn't have much but an old book that contained some of my thoughts written a long time ago. So now I am sending you this book of readings, meditations, and prayers. I hope that as you use it, you will be reminded that, although you go far from us, you will always be near to God, and God will never fail or forsake you, but will bring us all together to his joyful kingdom in good time. So we will pray for you and ask your prayers for us.

This book is not just from me but even more it is from this church, First Presbyterian Church, Kerrville, a congregation that has nurtured you, prayed over and with you, loved you through your growing up, and confirmed you in your faith. Sometimes the church has been compared to being a mother, and it is not a bad comparison. Mothers give us our births, labor to help us breathe, comfort us when we cry, feed us when we are hungry, help us learn to walk, teach us what is important in life. All of that this church has done in fulfilling the vows taken at your baptism, vows that are renewed at the baptism of every baby over whom we pour water. So does the church give birth to her children, laboring to help them breathe, wiping away their tears, feeding them word and sacrament, helping them learn how to walk straight and true, teaching them what is worthy of praise. And when our children are almost grown up, we push them out, wave goodbye, and watch them go off to college, knowing they are about to assume their own responsibilities. It's hard being a mother, wonderful at times, but also very hard. And yet, we would rather do this than anything else in the world. One day, you will understand.

In any case, we do not want you to leave without a gift, a book that reminds you from whence cometh our help. There are not enough readings and prayers in this book for the whole school year; these are meant only to get you started. All the readings are taken from the book of Psalms, and although there are 150 psalms, I have included only 30 here. Still, "praying the psalms" is how the church has often worshiped and it is an excellent way to "practice the presence of God."

The whole anatomy of the soul, John Calvin told us, is present in the Psalms—our longings, our hurts, our joys, our sorrows, our hopes, our fears. I suggest you first read the psalm for that day and then use the meditation as a way of entering your own time with God. Perhaps the best time for doing this is before the day has unfolded, but in any case, you will need some quiet time. I hope that as you read these psalms and pray these prayers, you remember the church that continues to love you and the Lord who has given you life and who has wonderful things for you to do in his world. Look to him, Kristin, and be radiant; so your face shall never be ashamed! (Ps. 34:5)

THOMAS W. CURRIE III
19 AUGUST, 1998
FIRST PRESBYTERIAN CHURCH, KERRVILLE, TEXAS

Prayers
for the
Road

Psalm 139 : 1-18

O Lord, you have searched me and known me.
You know when I sit down and when I rise up;
    You discern my thoughts from far away.
You search out my path and my lying down,
    And are acquainted with all my ways.
Even before a word is on my tongue,
    O Lord, you know it completely.
You hem me in, behind and before,
    And lay your hand upon me.
Such knowledge is too wonderful for me; it is so high
    that I cannot attain it.

Where can I go from your Spirit?
    Or where can I flee from your presence?
If I ascend to heaven, you are there;
    If I make my bed in Sheol, you are there.
If I take the wings of the morning and settle at the
    farthest limits of the sea,
    Even there your hand shall lead me, and your
    right hand shall hold me fast.
If I say, "Surely the darkness shall cover me,
    And the light around me become night,"
Even the darkness is not dark to you; the night is as
    bright as the day,
    For darkness is as light to you.

For it was you who formed my inward parts;
    You knit me together in my mother's womb.
I praise you, for I am fearfully and wonderfully
    made.

Wonderful are your works; that I know very well.
My frame was not hidden from you, when I was
being made in secret,
Intricately woven in the depths of the earth.
Your eyes beheld my unformed substance.
In your book were written all the days that were
formed for me,
When none of them as yet existed.
How weighty to me are your thoughts, O God!
How vast is the sum of them!
I try to count them—they are more than the sand;
I come to the end—I am still with you.

DAY I

PSALM 139

THIS PSALM TELLS US OF A LOVE THAT WE CANNOT OUT-
RUN. WHETHER WE FLY HIGHER THAN THE MOUNTAINS
OR DIVE DEEPER THAN THE SEA, WHETHER WE GO ALL
the way to China or just to college, "You are there!" The
psalmist found enormous comfort in the fact that God is
Lord away from home. You are leaving home. Sometimes
on Sunday morning in our home church, it is easy for us to
believe that God is Lord. God seems very real to us when
we are surrounded by those whom we love. But when you
are in a strange city or in college for the first time and you
are surrounded by strangers, new books, new ideas, new
ways of talking and being, it is easy to think you have left
God behind. For a while, that thought may even seem cool.
After all, you are not a child anymore: You are on your own.
Still, even adults who are "on their own" can get awfully lost
sometimes, and even terribly lonely. Very smart people can
lose their way. When that happens, when you are absolutely
convinced that you are lost and alone and it is all your fault,
then you find it all too easy to get down on yourself and
think God has written you off, too.

The psalmist believed that it was good news that no matter how low we get, we cannot get any lower than God. A
strange comfort, you think? Perhaps so, but if you did not
know it already, you must surely be discovering about now
that the best gifts God gives often look strange to us. When

Jesus cries out on the cross, "My God, my God, why have you forsaken me?" he is entering that Sheol of loneliness and abandonment of which the psalmist speaks. But he is also giving us a gift. He is going to the depths to meet us in the depths. He has been there before. Indeed, at the loneliest, lowest spot on earth, the one person we are liable to meet is God. And so, even when we think we are lonely or abandoned, we are not as alone as we think we are. "If I make my bed in Sheol, you are there."

God is the one we cannot escape. Your Presbyterian tradition has always known that in its bones, and that knowledge has been a strength. When others have thought that our problem is that we cannot find God—perhaps because we have ascended too high to be bothered with something as simpleminded as faith, or perhaps because we have descended too low to think ourselves worthy of his attention—our tradition has said that neither of these things is the real problem. The real problem is that we cannot escape God. Like a dog who will not go home, God follows us to school; like "a hound of heaven," he chases us "down the arches of the years."[1]

So remember this first day of school: God is with us. That is Jesus' name: Emannuel, God with us. He is with you this first day, and he will be with you every day, even at the end of your days.

Let us pray: For my mother and father and all my parents in the faith, receive my thanks, O Lord. They have loved me along the way and loved me at times when I was not very lovable. Thank you for giving them to me. And now, this day, help me to do my best to live as one who knows that Jesus Christ is Lord and that no one can outrun his love or defeat his grace. Help me to be glad in this day, to rejoice in the opportunities that come my way, to be open to new friends,

---

1. Francis Thompson, "The Hound of Heaven," in *Modern British Poetry*, ed. Louis Untermeyer (New York: Harcourt Brace & World, 1958), 86.

new ideas, new occasions of service, confident that all ways of truth lead back to Jesus Christ, who is the way, the truth, and the life. Lead me in his way, I pray, O Lord, for in that way I was brought up, and in that way I have found the God who has searched me and known me and still loves me. In Christ's name. Amen.

NOTES

Psalm 23

The Lord is my shepherd, I shall not want.
He makes me lie down in green pastures;
  He leads me beside still waters;
  He restores my soul.
He leads me in right paths for his name's sake.

Even though I walk through the darkest valley,
  I fear no evil;
For you are with me;
  Your rod and your staff—
  They comfort me.

You prepare a table before me
  In the presence of my enemies;
You anoint my head with oil;
  My cup overflows.
Surely goodness and mercy
  Shall follow me
All the days of my life,
And I shall dwell in the house of the Lord
  My whole life long.

DAY 2

PSALM 23

A "PSALM OF DAVID," WE ARE TOLD, IS PERHAPS THE MOST BELOVED OF ALL PSALMS. THE COMPARISON IS SO SIMPLE: "THE LORD IS MY SHEPHERD." SO I MUST BE HIS SHEEP. HE pastures me in green pastures and leads me beside still waters. He cares for me. He watches over me. But even more than that, he "restores my soul." Sheep get lost and frightened and discouraged. It is easy for them to think no one cares or even knows of their trouble. David reminds us that the Lord "restores my soul." He finds me in all my lostness and fills me with good things. And then he leads me. This may be the most profound statement of faith any of us can ever make: He leads me. It suggests that we are not our own, that despite our inclinations and desires, we cannot lead ourselves, for when we do, we always get lost. No, he leads me. We are not our own but belong to another who leads us.

When you were in Confirmation Class, you had to memorize the answer to the first question of the Heidelberg Catechism: "What is your only comfort in life and in death?" Do you remember how the answer began? "That I belong—body and soul, in life and in death—not to myself, but to my faithful Savior Jesus Christ." That answer is the gospel in miniature. We need not invent or reinvent ourselves or even submit to a series of self-contrived makeovers, for that heavy burden has been lifted from us. You are a gift. You are a gift that belongs to Jesus Christ, and he has made you and loves you. And in his image he is leading you to a fuller humanity. You do not belong to money or sex or power; you do not belong to the approval of others or to the culture's images of success or failure. You belong to Jesus. You are his sheep. That may not sound terribly glamorous or even very complimentary, but if you can receive yourself as such a gift, you will have received the whole gospel.

He leads us. David knows that to be led like this is not to be free of all suffering or trouble. One of the places "he leads us" is that "darkest valley," the valley of the shadow of death. Even there, he leads us. We think, sometimes, that following Jesus is like joining a club and, as such, may involve some duties, some dues, but not much more. We do not think it will involve our life. We do not think it will cause us to reflect on something as serious as our own death. But the reason you were given a Bible at your Confirmation was that those who welcomed you into the church knew you needed something more than "a lick and a promise" as you began your pilgrimage of faith. You needed a "weapon of the Spirit," indeed, spiritual armor, for you would likely encounter dragons and other wild beasts on your journey. Following Jesus Christ often brings us face to face with our own demons and those of our own culture. The Christian life is regularly involved in a kind of death struggle with idols we cherish, idols of our own making. We do not think that the Christian life requires a kind of dying, but that is just the way Jesus describes what it means to follow him. "If anyone would come after me, let him deny himself and take up his cross and follow me." So finding ourselves being led "through the darkest valley" should never surprise Christians. That is where Jesus spends a good deal of his time. That is where he leads us and where we confront our real enemies and find our real struggles.

That is where, if you permit me to say it, we grow up. The problem with so much that passes for Christianity today is that it is childish. It wants Jesus, but it does not want to venture into that "darkest valley," even if he does lead us there. It wants Jesus, but it does not want the hard work of loving the neighbors. It wants Jesus, but it does not want to have to serve on a committee or work in the church or reach out to one of the least of these. So we never grow up because we never die. We remain stuck in a selfish and silly Christianity.

David knew better. He knew that there is no following of God that does not sooner or later bring us to that "darkest valley." But that prospect did not frighten him. For the good news is that in that "valley," "you are with me." Paul asks in his letter to the Romans whether anything can finally defeat God's purpose in the world or separate us from the love of Christ. He mentions several possibilities: trouble, distress, persecution, famine, poverty, danger, death—all things one encounters in that "darkest valley." But he concludes that none of these things can do what they want to do. What they want to do is to defeat God's plan and purpose for you and for this creation. They want to separate you from his love. And that is the one thing they cannot do. "For I am sure that neither death, nor life, nor angels, nor principalities, nor things present, nor things to come, nor powers, nor height, nor depth, nor anything else in all creation will be able to separate us from the love of God in Christ Jesus our Lord." That is why the angels in the gospel stories so often tell us: "Do not be afraid." Do not be afraid. Jesus wins. He is with us.

The French mathematician, philosopher, and man of faith, Blaise Pascal, once wrote that "the heart has reasons that Reason knows not of."[2] The same could be said of the

2. Blaise Pascal, *Pensées* (London: Penguin Books, 1966), 154, #423.

good things faith enjoys. We do not live in a vale of tears, but enjoy tables spread before us in this life, blessings poured over our heads, "goodness and mercy" that follow us all our days. Faith has pleasures that Pleasure knows not of. Just so, faith is meant to be of great joy. The good shepherd intends for his sheep to be happy, and one day he will lead us into his eternal happiness, where we will "dwell in the house of the Lord" our "whole life long."

Let us pray: Help us to hear the good news of the gospel, Lord. Help us not to be afraid. Give us the courage to follow the good shepherd all our days, until we follow him into your kingdom. We pray this prayer in the name of Jesus Christ. Amen.

NOTES

Psalm 1

Happy are those who do not follow the advice of the
*   wicked,*
*   Or take the path that sinners tread,*
*   Or sit in the seat of scoffers;*
*   But their delight is in the law of the Lord,*
*   And on his law they meditate day and night.*
They are like trees planted by streams of water,
*   Which yield their fruit in its season,*
*   And their leaves do not wither.*
In all that they do, they prosper.

The wicked are not so, but are like chaff that the
*   wind drives away.*
Therefore the wicked will not stand in the judgment,
*   Nor sinners in the congregation of the righteous;*
For the Lord watches over the way of the righteous,
*   But the way of the wicked will perish.*

DAY 3

—∙—

PSALM 1

THE BOOK OF PSALMS BEGINS WITH THE PORTRAYAL OF PEOPLE WHO ARE WISE. THEY MAY NOT BE WISE IN TERMS OF FINANCIAL ACUMEN OR ACADEMIC BRILLIANCE, BUT they are wise in what matters: They are wise in the matter of living a fruitful and honorable life. "They," the psalmist says, "are like trees planted by streams of water."

It is easy for us to think that smarts are the only thing that matters. "Just do it," says Nike. "Winning cures cancer," said a football coach. "Just win, baby," said another. Our culture tells us that if you win, nothing else matters. And we believe that. We may want to "be like Mike," when we play basketball, but we do not need role models for daily life. Winning takes care of everything; winning justifies us no matter what we do. A talented athlete is arrested on a drug charge or for beating up a girlfriend or worse. Gifted politicians and preachers cannot remain faithful to their spouses or to their own promises. The careers of movie stars and celebrities soar even as their lives are in total disarray. And then we begin to think that perhaps there is a cost to such "winning," to such "justification."

When the psalmist contrasts all of this by comparing wise people to trees, it does not sound like much of an honor. The wise person, the psalmist insists, is "like a tree planted by streams of water." What does he mean? Why does the book of Psalms begin here?

Trees are rooted things: They bend, but they do not often break. To be like a tree is not to be uprooted by every fashion that blows in or every appetite that demands to be filled. A tree is stable: To be like a tree is to be faithful. The book of Psalms begins here because it wants us to know that the fruitful life, the truly good life, is not built on appetite or fashion but on faithfulness: on showing up, on doing your work, on keeping your promises. That is wisdom, and that wisdom is rooted in God's gift to us in his word. God shows up. God is faithful. His trees grow strong in the soil of his loving faithfulness, in the sunshine of his worship. There his "pleasant planting," his trees, are watered by grace and cultivated in love.

But a tree also offers shade. We need trees to stand under, to give us shade from the heat, places to rest awhile. Trees are examples. None of us can live without a model or an example. We may find them, as Mark Twain found them, "annoying," but in part that is because they remind us that we are not self-sufficient creatures. The question is not whether we follow an example; we do. The question is which one. Whom do we wish to stand beside? The wise person is one who has chosen to rest under the shade of God's tree. Such a person delights in God's word and has the courage to turn away from cheap imitations of life, even when they appear attractive and popular. The wise person is a person of courage. He or she is like a tree, and sometimes that means that he or she must stand alone, or more often, stand with other faithful people who are not afraid to claim the role of being a witness, an example to follow. We laugh at "good examples," but the psalmist does not. He thinks we need them.

Finally, there is a connection in being "like a tree" and in being true. The two words are connected in their Anglo-Saxon rootage, and the connection consists in the simple fact that a tree is a deeply rooted thing.[3] Its unyielding qual-

3. Eugene Peterson, *Answering God: The Psalms as a Tool for Prayer* (New York: Harper & Row, 1989), 27.

ity reflects the hard and unyielding nature of reality itself. There is nothing dreamlike about a tree. If you run into it, you are the one to stop. You must go around a tree or dig it up. It is principled, steadfast, deeply rooted, true. Its roots sustain a life that is able to lift its branches to heaven in the praise of God. The wicked are not so rooted in reality. They reflect a rootless culture. And before long, the cheap wear out; the slick do not show up, and they soon wither and die. To be true, as a person, is to be like a tree, deeply rooted in the soil of God's grace. That is where one begins in college, and in life, with the grace that roots us in God's story and enables us to offer praise and shade, nourishment and fruit, to an otherwise dry and withered land.

Let us pray: Grant me your truth, O Lord, that I may grow strong in the faith. Help me not to be afraid of being an example of Christ's love in the world. So may I learn to tell the truth with my life, following him who is the way, the truth and the life, even Jesus Christ. Amen.

Psalm 107 : 1-16; 39-43

O give thanks to the Lord, for he is good; for his
  steadfast love endures forever.
Let the redeemed of the Lord say so, those he
  redeemed from trouble
    And gathered in from the lands, from the east and
    from the west,
    From the north and from the south.

Some wandered in desert wastes, finding no way to an
  inhabited town;
    Hungry and thirsty, their soul fainted within
    them.
Then they cried to the Lord in their trouble,
    And he delivered them from their distress;
He led them by a straight way, until they reached an
  inhabited town.
Let them thank the Lord for his steadfast love,
    For his wonderful works to humankind.
For he satisfies the thirsty, and the hungry he fills
    with good things.

Some sat in darkness and in gloom, prisoners in misery
  and in irons,
For they had rebelled against the words of God,
    And spurned the counsel of the Most High.
Their hearts were bowed down with hard labor;
    They fell down, with no one to help.
Then they cried to the Lord in their trouble,

And he saved them from their distress;
He brought them out of darkness and gloom, and
broke their bonds asunder.
Let them thank the Lord for his steadfast love,
For his wonderful works to humankind.
For he shatters the doors of bronze and cuts in two
the bars of iron.

When they are diminished and brought low
Through oppression, trouble, and sorrow,
He pours contempt on princes and makes them
wander in trackless wastes;
But he raises up the needy out of distress, and
makes their families like flocks.
The upright see it and are glad; and all wickedness
stops its mouth.
Let those who are wise give heed to these things,
And consider the steadfast love of the Lord.

DAY 4

~ ~

THE CHIEF VIRTUE OF THE CHRISTIAN LIFE IS GRATITUDE. "O GIVE THANKS TO THE LORD, FOR HE IS GOOD," THE PSALM-IST SINGS, "FOR HIS STEADFAST LOVE ENDURES FOREVER." I have always thought that gratitude was a difficult thing to work up. Like humility, it is a virtue that resists our application. The more humble we become, the more proud of our humility we are; the harder we work at being grate-ful, the less inclined are we to discern that life is a gift. Yet Israel was always astonished at the mystery of God's good-ness. Manna came in the wilderness, and Israel was saved from hunger. Deliverance from the Egyptians miraculously occurred, and Israel found herself walking on dry ground. Who parted the waters? Who fed the people when they were hungry? How did they survive so many defeats and losses and disasters and still flourish? In looking back over her history, Israel saw the providence of God time and again: Joseph, almost murdered by his brothers, becoming the means of their salvation; Moses, threatened with death as a child, with a price on his head as an adult, becoming Israel's great deliverer; David, not the oldest or tallest son of Jesse but a mere keeper of sheep, becoming Israel's great shepherd-king, warrior-poet. Were these things just acci-dental? Luck? Good fortune? No, Israel confessed, these things were not the result of Lady Luck. These were gifts from God. Indeed, Israel came to understand her whole life

as such a gift, a people who by rights should not have survived but who did so because God's love for her was steadfast. That is why Israel practiced so hard learning to say
"Thank you." "Thank you," was the story of her life.

It is a good practice to learn to say "Thank you," not just
good manners or polite behavior, but a practice through
which we come to understand ourselves as part of God's
people, gifts ourselves who owe our lives to God. You are a
gift. I do not mean by that that you are just talented (which
you are), but, rather, that your life is a mysterious and wondrous gift from God's own hands and that you belong to
him. Eric Liddell, the great Scottish sprinter, is reported to
have said that he ran because God made him fast, and when
he ran he could feel God's pleasure. His running became a
form of saying "Thank you," a way of praising God, a way of
inviting others to join in singing, "O give thanks to the Lord
for he is good; for his steadfast love endures forever."

That is why practicing gratitude is less a matter of virtu-
ously learning to say "Thank you" than of learning to worship, learning to sing. Practicing gratitude is always a
response to what God has done. He gives; we give thanks.
He is faithful; we believe. He commands; we follow. We love
only because he first loved us. Worship is the place we hear
of that love and learn to look beyond ourselves to the Lord
who had made all things well. Worship is where we learn to
sing. Being grateful is also a gift then, not something we
conjure up, but something we receive in the joy of receiv-
ing God's "steadfast love."

A friend of mine was the best athlete in my high school.
He was our quarterback in football, our point guard in basketball, a high jumper in track. A great natural athlete, he
excelled in everything. He went to the University of Texas
and spent most of his first year there getting drunk. After
one year, he dropped out and came home disgraced. Quietly,
he enrolled at the University of Houston, where, after a long

time of working and then going to school, he eventually graduated. He began attending worship at the church that raised him and found his life regaining a center. Those whom he had previously taken for granted now became sources of strength. They taught him how to sing again. Some time later, a much younger friend of his, who lived down the street and who admired him greatly, started playing football, too. He was not as talented as my friend, but he loved to play. One night he was badly injured in a game and required neck surgery. He never fully recovered and was paralyzed from the waist down. He went through treatment and therapy and eventually finished high school and college. He needed a companion, though, one who would help him negotiate the hallways and apartments and help him with his books. My friend volunteered for that job and for the next four years was his roommate and helper. They went to church together and found in the company of that community a life that shaped their own in thanksgiving and praise.

In some ways, my friend had lost everything: his skills, his fame, even some of his friends. But he found something better; he found a life of gratitude, a life whose mysterious goodness continued to astonish him. He was no "suffering saint," not even a Boy Scout. He was simply a person who had discovered what he was put on earth to do. His life, against all odds, had become a gift.

"O give thanks to the Lord, for he is good; for his stead-fast love endures forever."

Let us pray: O Lord, teach me your ways. Grant the gift of worship. Give me a grateful heart that I may discern your gifts and live happily as your child. In Christ's name I offer this prayer. Amen.

NOTES

Psalm 34

I will bless the Lord at all times;
  His praise shall continually be in my mouth.
My soul makes its boast in the Lord; let the humble
  hear and be glad.
O magnify the Lord with me, and let us exalt his
  name together.

I sought the Lord, and he answered me, and delivered
  me from all my fears.
Look to him and be radiant; so your faces shall never
  be ashamed.
This poor soul cried, and was heard by the Lord,
  And was saved from every trouble.
The angel of the Lord encamps around those who
  fear him, and delivers them.
O taste and see that the Lord is good; happy are
  those who take refuge in him.
O fear the Lord, you his holy ones, for those who fear
  him have no want.
The young lions suffer want and hunger,
  But those who seek the Lord lack no good thing.

Come, O children, listen to me; I will teach you the
  fear of the Lord.
Which of you desires life, and covets many days to
  enjoy good?
Keep your tongue from evil, and your lips from
  speaking deceit.
Depart from evil, and do good; seek peace, and
  pursue it.

The eyes of the Lord are on the righteous,
    And his ears are open to their cry.
The face of the Lord is against evildoers,
    To cut off the remembrance of them from the
    earth.
When the righteous cry for help, the Lord hears,
    And rescues them from all their troubles.
The Lord is near to the brokenhearted, and saves the
    crushed in spirit.

Many are the afflictions of the righteous,
    But the Lord rescues them from them all.
He keeps all their bones; not one of them will be
    broken.
Evil brings death to the wicked,
    And those who hate the righteous will be
    condemned.
The Lord redeems the life of his servants;
    None of those who take refuge in him will be
    condemned.

DAY 5

—•—

PSALM 34

WE ALL HAVE OUR FAVORITE PSALMS. THIS IS MINE. TWO VERSES HAVE ALWAYS STRUCK ME AS PARTICULARLY BEAUTIFUL. THE FIRST IS VERSE 5: "LOOK TO HIM AND be radiant; so your faces shall never be ashamed." The psalmist is reminding Israel from whence cometh her help, just as his words remind the church today of the sun that shines on us in the Son, Jesus Christ. "Look to him and be radiant." Look to this Son. When we look to Jesus Christ, we truly shine; we truly reflect our purpose. Our culture tells us daily of the importance of looking to ourselves. Look to yourself for your own salvation, for your own good, for your own pleasure. I, I am assured, am the center of my world. Yet, when I become the center of my world, my world has a way of becoming a very small place indeed. After awhile, this small place, "my turf," becomes a kingdom that I must defend, and I soon become resentful of others' claims. Looking to myself, far from making me radiant, only makes me lonely and fearful and small. What our culture calls freedom is so often a kind of hell, a small, miserable, lonely place.

The gospel tells us something that seems almost absurd to our culture. It tells us that we are not the center of the world, that we have been displaced and are in fact, "displaced persons." For many, this comes as only bad news. Having worked so hard to be at the center, we take no pleasure in hearing that the world does not revolve around us. But just so does the gospel wound to heal. Christ the center helps us find our rightful place in his service, in his life. I tell you there is no happier discovery than learning that we no longer have to be the center of our own little worlds. It is the most marvelous gift to look to him for that center and to find our life in the largeness of his life.

Occasionally, I suffer from a black depression. I do not think it is life threatening, but it is a "thorn in the flesh," something I wish would simply go away but rarely does, at least not without a struggle. I suspect many folk face such a threat and, no doubt, deal with it better than I do. But when I am really low, I often fall into conversation with God, asking him why things cannot be a little different or why I must bear this particular burden. Sometimes, what saves me from total blackness is the slow but dawning realization that I am not as important as I think I am; I am not even the center of my own life. That may sound to you a bit contrived, a bit too "humble," or even a bit sick, but what I mean is that one of the symptoms of living as if you were at the center of the universe is that you stew over yourself a good deal. After all, the world seems curiously resistant to the knowledge that I am at the center of things, so that it takes a lot of stewing to "explain myself." Another way of putting this is to observe that sometimes my "black moods" reflect a self-centeredness, the inevitable result of taking myself too seriously. That is why the birds of the air and the lilies of the field are never depressed. They never suffer from the illusion that they are the center of things. They can simply offer praise happily and gladly to their center in God.

"Look to him," the psalmist tells us, "and be radiant." Be joyful, happy, radiant, not because you must invent or explain yourself, but because God has lifted that burden from you. Rejoice in his "Sonshine" and in his light receive yourself anew. "Come unto me," Jesus says, "all you who stew and are deeply anxious about yourselves, and I will give you rest. Take my yoke upon you; center yourself on my cross and learn of me, and you will find rest for your soul." "Look to him and be radiant, and your face will never be ashamed."

The second verse I have always loved is Verse 8: "O taste and see that the Lord is good; happy are those who take refuge in him."

God is good. The Christian faith is no great achievement, not even a moral triumph. It is a gift. That is what we have so much trouble believing. We are always looking for the catch. A gift? We would almost prefer it to be an achievement. That way we could control it. But it resists all our efforts to do so and insists on coming to us as a gift. In the fifth century, Saint Augustine compared the gospel to a man holding out his hand to receive a gift of rice. Most of us, Augustine said, rather than holding our hands out, hold out our clenched fists. We are so afraid of losing our grip on ourselves that we cannot even open our hands to receive what God intends to give us. That man is blessed, Augustine thought, who can turn himself loose long enough to open his hand to God and receive the most marvelous gift of his own humanity in Jesus Christ.

Why go to church? Why pray? Why seek to become something more than a mere consumer blown about by every fad of getting and spending? Perhaps it is a way of opening our hands to receive the gift.

Let us pray: Intrude on my life, O Lord, with your gracious gifts, that I might look to you and ever be radiant, ever reflecting your light. Save me from self-importance, and give me the laughter that birds of the air and lilies of the field seem to know so well. Then may I taste and see your goodness in Jesus Christ, finding in him "the sweet life," the unanxious life of his kingdom. I offer this prayer not in my own strength but freely in the name of Jesus Christ. Amen.

NOTES

Psalm 127

Unless the Lord builds the house, those who build it
*   labor in vain.*
Unless the Lord guards the city, the guard keeps
*   watch in vain.*
It is in vain that you rise up early and go late to rest,
*   Eating the bread of anxious toil;*
*   For he gives sleep to his beloved.*

Sons are indeed a heritage from the Lord,
*   The fruit of the womb a reward.*
Like arrows in the hand of a warrior are the sons of
*   one's youth.*
Happy is the man who has his quiver full of them.
He shall not be put to shame when he speaks with
*   his enemies in the gate.*

DAY 6

—◆◆—

PSALM 127

THIS PSALM IS ABOUT BEGINNINGS AND ENDINGS. "UNLESS THE LORD BUILDS THE HOUSE, THOSE WHO BUILD IT LABOR IN VAIN." THAT IS WHERE WE BEGIN. WE ASK GOD'S blessing before we eat a meal. At the beginning of worship, we confess at the outset that "Our help is in the name of the Lord." If it were not, how would we ever be able to worship? When I was a child, before we started on long trips, my father would lead us in prayer for a safe journey. Before any significant undertaking, whether we are building a church or a life or starting a new semester in college, we run the risk of working in vain, especially if we think that our building or our schooling or our living begins with ourselves. What the psalmist sees is that such undertakings invite us to enter into God's working, to receive the foundation he has laid, to build in the beginning he has made with us in Jesus Christ. In our baptism, we recall the beginning God has made. All of our life and all of our life's work are to be lived with this beginning in mind.

But the psalmist has more in mind than simply asking God's blessing on our work. He knows that there are times when we do not work so hard or cannot work, times when we fail or fall or even go to sleep. Who watches over us then, especially when we cannot do so ourselves? If we began with ourselves, we would be in trouble. We would not even be able to fall asleep, for while we were sleeping, we would be especially vulnerable. The truth is, however, our bodies do fail, every day. We need rest, and we need sleep. Each day is a kind of life: In the morning the day is young, but as the sun creeps slowly westward, the day grows older and eventually is laid to rest. The next morning brings a resurrection, a new day to us, but who watches over us while we sleep? "Unless the Lord watches over the city, the watchman stays awake in vain. It is in vain that you rise up early and go late to rest, eating the bread of anxious toil; for he gives sleep to his beloved." God watches over us. We do not begin with ourselves but with him. When we fail, he does not. "He gives sleep to his beloved."

When I was a first-year student in college, I struggled with a chemistry course. And I mean I struggled. Toward the end of the semester and before a big test, I decided that I would "pull an all-nighter," hoping, I think, that my hard work and good intentions would somehow translate into a higher mark. I made it until about 2:30 A.M. and then fell asleep. The next day there were so many cobwebs in my head that I did no better on the test and probably a bit worse. I had worked so hard, but all in vain. I did not think then of sleep as a gift, something like Sabbath rest, which God had given me for my own good. I thought I was in the possession of my own life and could build this house on my own. Sleep was a sign of weakness, really an embarrassment. But my body knew something my mind had forgotten, namely, that I was not made for my own plans but for communion with God, made to rest in him. "He gives sleep to his beloved."

Now, I am aware that the gift of sleep can be abused. When I was in college, I also slept through some classes I should have attended. And when I did that, God did not protect me from the consequences. But the refusal to sleep or to find in it a blessing is in some ways a refusal to accept our own humanity, the gift of the life God has made for us in Jesus Christ. The psalm, which reminds us how we should begin ("Unless the Lord builds the house, those who build it labor in vain."), also tells us how to end each day ("for he gives sleep to his beloved"). He watches over you. Even when you are unable to watch over yourself, when you are asleep and have "died" as the day has died, even then he watches over you and gives you rest and raises you to a new day of life with him. It is a blessing to enter into this labor and to enter into this rest, and above all, to enter into this life.

Let us pray: Give me the grace to begin this day aright, O Lord. And be with me as the day wears on, in my studies and in my work, in my speaking and in my listening. And be with me, I pray, at the end of this day, particularly in my resting and in my sleep, that I might rise to a life of praise and thanksgiving at the new day that is to come. In Christ's name, I pray. Amen.

Psalm 27

The Lord is my light and my salvation; whom shall I
*   fear?*
The Lord is the stronghold of my life; of whom shall I
*   be afraid?*

When evildoers assail me to devour my flesh—
*   My adversaries and foes—they shall stumble and*
*   fall.*

Though an army encamp against me, my heart shall
*   not fear;*
Though war rise up against me, yet I will be
*   confident.*

One thing I asked of the Lord, that will I seek after:
To live in the house of the Lord all the days of my
*   life,*
To behold the beauty of the Lord, and to inquire in
*   his temple.*

For he will hide me in his shelter in the day of
*   trouble;*
*   He will conceal me under the cover of his tent; he*
*   will set me high on a rock.*

Now my head is lifted up above my enemies all
*   around me,*
*   And I will offer in his tent sacrifices with shouts*
*   of joy;*
I will sing and make melody to the Lord.

Hear, O Lord, when I cry aloud, be gracious to me
   and answer me!
"Come," my heart says, "seek his face!"
   Your face, Lord, do I seek. Do not hide your face
   from me.

Do not turn your servant away in anger, you who
   have been my help.
Do not cast me off, do not forsake me, O God of my
   salvation!
If my father and mother forsake me, the Lord will
   take me up.

Teach me your way, O Lord, and lead me on a level
   path because of my enemies.
Do not give me up to the will of my adversaries,
   For false witnesses have risen against me, and
   they are breathing out violence.

I believe that I shall see the goodness of the Lord in
   the land of the living.
Wait for the Lord; be strong and let your heart take
   courage;
   Wait for the Lord!

DAY 7

~ ~

PSALM 27

"T HE LORD IS MY LIGHT AND MY SALVATION; WHOM SHALL I FEAR? THE LORD IS THE STRONGHOLD OF MY LIFE; OF WHOM SHALL I BE AFRAID?"

It is remarkable how often the psalmists speak of fear, of being afraid. We do not talk much about such things. Occasionally we speak of being fearful of a big exam or of painful surgery or of a potential calamity, but these things are not our enemies so much as they are simply "the natural shocks that flesh is heir to." Being afraid is something else.

When I was in the seventh grade, I was afraid almost every day. A fellow who was a bully picked on the same person for several days in a row, hoping to provoke a fight and, in the meantime, enjoying the misery of someone not as strong as he. I hated him, in part because I knew I would lose in any fight with him, but I also hated him because he was cruel. He enjoyed watching others suffer. One day he started in on me, and for the next several weeks my life was miserable. I suspect that the closest I ever came to understanding the psalmist's plight was when I was in the seventh grade and felt that I indeed had an adversary and foe, that I had good reason to fear.

I wish I could report that I prayed to God and then, miraculously, all my problems were solved. Indeed, I did pray, but as I recall, my shirts were still ripped, my books knocked to the floor, my lunch often stolen. What eventually happened was that we both grew up a bit. He grew tired of tormenting others, and we found ourselves on the same basketball team. Eventually, we even became friends and studied together for a while. During all this time, however, I remember having to struggle to go to school. I did not want to see him, and I hated myself for being afraid. One day I decided that I just did not care. I was tired of being afraid, and if I got beat up, I got beat up. I remember even thinking that God would have to watch over me; I was putting my future in his hands. Whether because of my new resolve or simply because things changed, life got better after that. The road did not become suddenly smooth, but somehow I was better able to negotiate the bumps.

In retrospect, I am embarrassed to talk about all this with you, except that it is so difficult for us today to admit to ever having an "enemy." Such an admission risks revealing us to be not very "nice" people, angry or conflicted or even "negative." But when you are a child, an "enemy" is a very real concept. Children know an "enemy" when they see one.

A friend of mine is dying of cancer. She has fought this bully for five years, and she has fought him well. Just when it looks as if this enemy has got her down, she finds a way to parry his attack and escape his clutches. Courage is a virtue that we sometimes associate with soldiers or athletes, but I have never known a more courageous person than this woman who is fighting for her life. What enables her to negotiate not just the bumps but the defeats and the losses she has sustained?

One day, when I was sitting at her bedside, she asked me to read her a psalm. "The Lord is my light and my salvation," I read, "whom shall I fear?" "The Lord is the stronghold of my life; of whom shall I be afraid?" She turned to me and said, "Faith gives me courage to fight. I hate bullies, and this damned disease is a bully and may well eventually lick me. But it will not win. It will not win. Jesus wins."

The reason I am sending you this book of meditations and prayers is to give you a weapon of the Spirit against all bullies. They do not win. Even when they appear to win, they do not. Even when they threaten to take our lives, they do not win. Jesus wins. The cross wins. The crucified Lord whom the bullies thought they had killed—he wins. In his company and by his grace, no foe can destroy what he has won. The bully always wants to think he can determine our lives and even the meaning of our deaths, but he cannot. For we belong to Jesus Christ, and dying we live in the terms of his Easter story. Therefore we are right to seek his face, confident that Christ will hide us in the day of trouble and will conceal us under the cover of his own tent. Then we will be lifted up in Christ, lifted up above all our enemies, offering with Christ our own sacrifices and shouts of joy. Faith in him gives us courage to live even in the face of our enemies. "The Lord is my light and my salvation; whom shall I fear? The Lord is the stronghold of my life; of whom shall I be afraid?"

Let us pray: Give me such strength, O Lord, such weapons of the Spirit, to live faithfully and courageously before my friends and enemies. Your face, Lord, would I seek, so that when frightened or anxious, I might always entrust myself to your care. In Christ's name, I pray this. Amen.

NOTES

Psalm 122

I was glad when they said to me,
  "Let us go to the house of the Lord!"
Our feet are standing within your gates, O Jerusalem.

Jerusalem—built as a city that is bound firmly
  together.
To it the tribes go up, the tribes of the Lord,
  As was decreed for Israel, to give thanks to the
  name of the Lord.
For there the thrones for judgment were set up,
  The thrones of the house of David.

Pray for the peace of Jerusalem:
  "May they prosper who love you. Peace be within
  your walls,
  And security within your towers."
For the sake of my relatives and friends I will say,
  "Peace be within you."
For the sake of the house of the Lord our God, I will
  seek your good.

DAY 8

PSALM 122

THIS PSALM BEGINS WITH THE WORDS: "I WAS GLAD WHEN THEY SAID TO ME, 'LET US GO TO THE HOUSE OF THE LORD!'" THE PSALM IS ABOUT THE TEMPLE IN JERUSALEM "to which the tribes go up," there "to give thanks to the name of the Lord." The psalm is about going to worship.

How could anyone be so glad about simply going to worship? Is it not a chore to get up on Sunday morning when we would much rather sleep late, have a late breakfast, read the paper, enjoy doing nothing? We deserve the rest, the time to let our minds and bodies vegetate awhile. The poet Wallace Stevens described in his poem "Sunday Morning" the happy contentment of a world that finds in Easter no special claim on its attention. It is a world we recognize, a world satisfied with "late coffee and oranges in a sunny chair."[4] What is so wrong with that?

Going to church takes work: It requires some preparation. Moreover, it is often lonely work. Our roommates, even our friends, might well not be so interested in this effort as we are. On the other hand, such work as it takes is not the usual work we do. We do not usually get all dressed up in the morning; we do not usually join with others in song and prayer; we do not usually give and receive

4. Wallace Stevens, "Sunday Morning," in *Modern American Poetry*, ed. Louis Untermeyer (New York: Harcourt Brace & World, 1958), 242.

hospitality and greetings; we do not usually listen to an old story told once again in our hearing. We do not usually receive bread and wine. No, going to church marks the day as special and imposes a structure on the day, a discipline on our lives. The week turns. And when we come home from church, we know something is different, just as we know something is deeply, deeply right. The week can begin now. We have been blessed and forgiven again and have offered our own songs of praise. And the truth of God's love for us in Jesus Christ has enfolded us yet again, and we have seen it, yet again, as the deepest truth of all, the truth that makes everything true and right.

Sometimes, when I go on vacations or long trips, I miss a Sunday and do not get to worship that day. In one sense, of course, it is a day like every other day. One cannot tell just by looking at it that the day is Sunday. But at the end of the day, when I finally realize that it is Sunday, I feel a bit displaced, cheated, sad. I have missed being with God's people and hearing with them the story of God's love for this world, the story that tells me my own. And I am unsettled.

Of course, you can get to the point where such unsettledness becomes so familiar that you grow content with it. That is what Wallace Stevens's poem is about, and in a way, that is what a completely secular life represents: contentment with a godless world. The problem is that even such contentment is difficult to sustain for very long, because in such a world, we become more and more the center of the life we seek to keep God out of. As G. K. Chesterton would tell us, the problem is not that we start believing in nothing; the problem is that we start believing in anything. Moreover, God is sneakier than we think is permissible, and he often seeps into places we thought were well sealed off.

"I was glad when they said to me, 'Let us go to the house of the Lord.'" One reason to go to church is to be fed by the bread that truly nourishes, to hear again the truth that Jesus

Christ is the center of our lives. In displacing us from that center, he tells us the best news of all: He tells us that we need not invent or reinvent ourselves. We need not pretend to be our own creators. Rather, we need only receive ourselves from his hand, become the forgiven sinners we are.

You cannot go very long without food, and it is no shame to admit that you are hungry. Why go to church? Because we are hungry. That is a good enough reason to be glad when people say to me, "Let us go to the house of the Lord." So may you be hungry all your life and find food at the table of our Lord Jesus Christ.

Let us pray: Help me, O Lord, to remember the Sabbath Day to keep it holy, to remember its strangeness, how unlike all the other days it is. Help me always to embrace that strangeness, to be glad to come to your table and be fed by your hand. In Jesus Christ's name. Amen.

Psalm 2

Why do the nations conspire, and the peoples plot in
  vain?
The kings of the earth set themselves, and the rulers
  take counsel together,
  Against the Lord and his anointed, saying,
  "Let us burst their bonds asunder, and cast their
  cords from us."

He who sits in the heavens laughs; the Lord has them
  in derision.
Then he will speak to them in his wrath, and terrify
  them in his fury, saying,
"I have set my king on Zion, my holy hill."

I will tell of the decree of the Lord: He said to me,
  "You are my son; today I have begotten you.
  Ask of me, and I will make the nations your heritage,
  And the ends of the earth your possession.
  You shall break them with a rod of iron,
  And dash them in pieces like a potter's vessel."

Now therefore, O kings, be wise; be warned, O rulers of
  the earth.
Serve the Lord with fear, with trembling kiss his feet,
  Or he will be angry, and you will perish in the way;
  For his wrath is quickly kindled.

Happy are all who take refuge in him.

DAY 9

PSALM 2

ECENTLY, BILL MAY, WHO TEACHES ETHICS AT SOUTHERN METHODIST UNIVERSITY, GAVE A SET OF LECTURES AT OUR CHURCH. ON THAT OCCASION, HE TOLD OF AN EXPERIENCE he had when he was invited on two successive weekends to speak first at New York University Business School and, second, at a monastery in Indiana. He had planned to deliver pretty much the same speech—on Christian ethics—at both places. At both places he was served lunch, but the way he was served lunch differed a good deal from one place to the other. At NYU, he sat in a large lunchroom full of business students. Some read the *The Wall Street Journal;* others read business magazines or studied books. Surrounding them on every side, projected on the walls just above eye level, was a running tape of the latest stock transactions on the New York Stock Exchange. The market was all around them. Whether the Dow-Jones was up or down was immediately apparent. That was the story of their lunchtime, and it promised to be the story of their lives.

At the monastery, things were different. The monks sat at long tables and ate just as the business students did, although perhaps the fare was a bit simpler. Instead of the Dow-Jones average broadcast on the walls of their lunchroom, the monks had one of their own reading from the Bible. They "ate" the word along with their food. It had become the story of their lives.

A German philosopher by the name of Ludwig Feuerbach once opined that "we are what we eat." He was right. Along with our food, we "eat" or take in narratives of hope or images of success, which shape the way we view ourselves. What are you eating? Which story are you listening to? The monks "ate" the Bible (like Ezekiel of old), hoping that that story would be digested and internalized and made into muscle and bone and put into Christ's service. The business school students also ate, and what they ate was not bad. There is nothing wrong in being ambitious, working hard, and wanting success. But when our ambitions become our staple diet, then we run the risk of gaining the whole world only to lose our souls. We are then eating a lie, because in truth, we belong not to ourselves or even to our ambitions, but to Jesus Christ.

The psalmist looked at his world and saw what people were eating. He saw how seriously the powerful took themselves. They were the kings and rulers of the earth. That was their story; that was what they ate. "Why do the nations conspire," the psalmist asks, "and the peoples plot in vain?" Do they think they are really in control of this world? Why do they eat such a lie? Do they not know it will give them indigestion? "He who sits in the heavens laughs; the Lord has them in derision."

An old saying has it that if you want to make God laugh, tell him your plans. When we read the newspapers or watch the television news, the plans we hear of are so impressive: plans of war, plans of murders, plans of nations, plans of "movers and shakers." Where is God in all of that? Usually, God is not mentioned in all of that. He seems, in such a context, small, almost like a child whom the powerful can afford to overlook. After all, how many legions does God have?

God is often overlooked. That was Israel's history. She was not the largest or most powerful of nations. More often, she was a pawn on the chessboard of much more powerful nations. Who needed to take Israel seriously? Yet Israel survived. The Jews, although scattered and often defeated, remained a people, and from their life and worship, the story that has become our story emerged. Marvelous to relate, Israel became the real story in history. What God promised to Abraham came true, namely, that all the nations blessed themselves through Israel's life.

That is the way God works. The gospel is never obvious or superficial; it is, rather, hidden. The glamour of the superficial does not last. What remains is what is hidden: a baby in swaddling clothes lying in a manger, overlooked by Caesar and all the other powers. They think they are writing "world history," only to discover that they are playing a role, a somewhat marginal role, in "his story."

So what? Well, so this. You will study the powerful in college. You will learn how to test and measure things; how to judge and think critically; how to take your place as a responsible member of society. All of which is well and good, and all of which deserves your very best efforts. But remember: Some things happen underground; some gifts are hidden; some events have quite unintended consequences; and some of the most important things are missed entirely; they are things that we often think are not important at all. It all depends on what you are eating, that is, on which story you are listening to: the one that envisions us as the center of the universe or the one that leads to the praise and worship of God. Which story are you listening to? What are you eating? Do not be ashamed of what is small; do not dismiss the underground. That is where Christians once worshiped and that is where God is characteristically at work even today, hidden from the powerful, slowly transforming the world.

Let us pray: Give me perspective, Lord, that I might laugh. Teach me to laugh at what should be laughed at: the making of idols, the pretense of self-worship, the lust for power. Grant me the gift of true worship, I pray, that I might join in your laughter and come to rejoice in him who holds the whole world in his hands. Help me to find that blessing that comes to all who take refuge in the laughter and the joy of Jesus Christ. In his name, I pray. Amen.

NOTES

Psalm 42

*As a deer longs for flowing streams, so my soul longs
for you, O God.*
My soul thirsts for God, for the living God.
When shall I come and behold the face of God?
My tears have been my food day and night,
*While people say to me continually, "Where is
your God?"*

These things I remember, as I pour out my soul:
How I went with the throng,
And led them in procession to the house of God,
*With glad shouts and songs of thanksgiving, a
multitude keeping festival.*
*Why are you cast down, O my soul, and why are you
disquieted within me?*
*Hope in God; for I shall again praise him, my help
and my God.*

My soul is cast down within me;
*Therefore I remember you from the land of Jordan
and of Hermon,*
From Mount Mizar.
Deep calls to deep at the thunder of your cataracts;
All your waves and your billows have gone over me.
By day the Lord commands his steadfast love,
*And at night his song is with me, a prayer to the
God of my life.*

I say to God, my rock, "Why have you forgotten me?
  Why must I walk about mournfully because the
  enemy oppresses me?"
As with a deadly wound in my body, my adversaries
  taunt me,
  While they say to me continually, "Where is your
  God?"

Why are you cast down, O my soul, and why are you
  disquieted within me?
Hope in God; for I shall again praise him, my help
  and my God.

DAY 10

❧ ❧

PSALM 42

THIS PSALM IS ABOUT BEING HOMESICK. I DO NOT KNOW WHETHER YOU HAVE BEEN AWAY FROM HOME LONG ENOUGH TO BE HOMESICK. IN FACT, YOU MAY BE FEELING just the opposite: delighting in finally being on your own. In any case, sooner or later we all get homesick, if not for the home we knew, at least for the home we long for.

"As a deer longs for flowing streams, so my soul longs for you, O God. . . . My tears have been my food day and night, while people say to me continually, 'Where is your God?'" This psalmist knows what it is like to be lonely in the midst of a crowd, to be odd when everyone else is comfortably the same. He is surrounded by folk who do not take his faith seriously, who offer him little or no support in his believing. He has grown tired, weary with his own oddness. He longs to taste again what once seemed in such abundant supply: the joy of being with others in worship. "These things I remember as I pour out my soul: how I went with the throng, and led them in procession to the house of God, with glad shouts and songs of thanksgiving, a multitude keeping festival." Those were the days. Then the psalmist was surrounded by a "multitude" of friends and family; then he was not odd or different, but part of a "throng"; then he led them all in a procession. Then worship was easier.

One of the things about being on your own is learning to take counsel with yourself. In some ways, that is part of what it means to grow up: to make your own decisions, to be responsible for your own judgments. But we soon learn that can be lonely work, especially when our judgment differs from that of our peers. Adults often think peer pressure applies only to children or teenagers, but in fact, it operates even more fiercely later on. For example, it is possible to feel alone in college. On such occasions, we long for company: for God, for our families, for our friends, even for our churches. We remember how comfortable and warm worship at home seemed. "As a deer longs for flowing streams, so my soul longs for you, O God." And we ask ourselves, "Why are you cast down, O my soul, and why are you disquieted within me?" I remember Sunday mornings in college as being some of the loneliest times in my life, recalling as I did, my family, my church, my home, so far away. On a day that should have been a happy day, I was often miserable, vulnerable to a homesickness of the heart.

I think Christians often feel homesick. I think that is part of the deal, part of what it means to be Christian. In the fifth century, Saint Augustine began his *Confessions* with this prayer: "For thou hast made us for thyself and restless is our heart until it comes to rest in thee."[5] If our hearts are truly made for God, then we are always homesick for the one who made us and redeemed us. True, we often try to salve this homesickness for God with other things: going shopping, manipulating other people, distracting ourselves with endless entertainment, losing ourselves in the labyrinth of sexual freedom. But in the end, nothing satisfies. Our hearts remain restless, ever homesick, until they rest in God. We

5. Saint Augustine, *The Confessions,* Vol. 17 of The Library of Christian Classics, ed. Albert Outler (Philadelphia: Westminster Press, 1955), 31.

long for heaven. I do not mean we long for harps and clouds and sweetness and light, but that we long for God.

Recently, I was reading a book about medieval cathedrals in which the author claimed that the medieval cathedral was thought at the time to be a heavenly embassy on earth. Today, when our country establishes an embassy in a foreign country, the land on which that embassy sits becomes the territory of the United States, subject to the laws of our government. It is, if you will, a little piece of the United States in a foreign nation. The medieval cathedral was thought of in much the same way: a colony of heaven on earth, a place where God's kingdom intruded on our realm and became officially his property, subject to his laws. To this embassy, faithful "strangers and exiles" on earth could repair, be fitted with their passports, and begin their pilgrimage to that heavenly city that is our true home. That is why pilgrims visited such places of worship, because such places helped them find their way home.

The psalmist offers an answer to his own question, "Why are you cast down, and why are you disquieted within me?" "Hope in God," he says, "for I shall again praise him, my help and my God." Hope in God.

That may not seem like much of an answer, but, in fact, hope has always been the baggage that pilgrims carry. Hope has ever been the transportation that has carried pilgrims and their baggage. We live by hope. Hope in God. Hope is how pilgrims find their way to the embassy, find their way to the sanctuary, find their way home. Hope leads us to worship, to God's people, without whom we can neither learn to hope nor become a Christian. When we worship with them, we are gathered in the Spirit, gathered with all those whom we have loved, and we walk, once again with them, "a throng," "a multitude keeping festival." What is the cure for homesickness? Worship. Worship is the place where we learn to hope, the place where our restless hearts at last find rest in God.

Let us pray: Give me strength, O Father, not to be afraid to stand alone. But give me the help of other people, I pray, who stand with me before you. Receive my thanks for all those who have led me to worship. Bless them this day, I pray. And grant to us all such hope in you that our longing might be fulfilled in lives that are faithful and pleasing to you. I offer this prayer in the name of him who has ever stood by me, even Jesus Christ. Amen.

Psalm 22 : 1-24

My God, my God, why have you forsaken me?
  Why are you so far from helping me, from the
  words of my groaning?
O my God, I cry by day, but you do not answer; and
  by night, but find no rest.

Yet you are holy, enthroned on the praises of Israel.
In you our ancestors trusted; they trusted, and you
    delivered them.
To you they cried, and were saved;
In you they trusted, and were not put to shame.

But I am a worm, and not human; scorned by others,
    and despised by the people.
All who see me mock at me; they make mouths at me,
    they shake their heads;
"Commit your cause to the Lord; let him deliver—
    Let him rescue the one in whom he delights!"

Yet it was you who took me from the womb;
  You kept me safe on my mother's breast.
On you I was cast from my birth,
    And since my mother bore me you have been my
    God.
Do not be far from me, for trouble is near and there
    is no one to help.

Many bulls encircle me, strong bulls of Bashan
  surround me;

They open wide their mouths at me, like a
ravening and roaring lion.

I am poured out like water, and all my bones are out
of joint;
My heart is like wax; it is melted within my breast;
My mouth is dried up like a potsherd,
And my tongue sticks to my jaws; you lay me in the
dust of death.

For dogs are all around me; a company of evildoers
encircles me.
My hands and feet have shriveled; I can count all
my bones.
They stare and gloat over me; they divide my
clothes among themselves,
And for my clothing they cast lots.

But you, O Lord, do not be far away! O my help,
come quickly to my aid!
Deliver my soul from the sword, my life from the
power of the dog!
Save me from the mouth of the lion!

From the horns of the wild oxen you have rescued me.
I will tell of your name to my brothers and sisters;
In the midst of the congregation I will praise you:
You who fear the Lord, praise him! All you offspring
of Jacob, glorify him;

Stand in awe of him, all you offspring of Israel!
For he did not despise or abhor the affliction of the
    afflicted;
    He did not hide his face from me, but heard when
    I cried to him.

DAY 11

 ⸺•⸺

PSALM 22

THE ONE BOOK OF THE OLD TESTAMENT THAT IS QUOTED MORE IN THE NEW TESTAMENT THAN ANY OTHER IS THE BOOK OF PSALMS. THIS PARTICULAR PSALM BEGINS WITH the words Jesus utters on the cross: "My God, my God, why have you forsaken me?" If you read the whole psalm, you see other phrases or images that have made their way into the Passion story. For example, Verses 16 through 18: "For dogs are all around me; a company of evildoers encircles me. My hands and feet have shriveled; I can count all my bones. They stare and gloat over me; they divide my clothes among themselves, and for my clothing they cast lots."

This is a frightening psalm. It is the cry of one who feels utterly abandoned. And it is a cry whose anguish is hurled at God: "*My* God, *my* God, why have *you* forsaken me?" It is hard for us to hear such anguish today. It is hard in part because to hear it is so painful, but also because we think we need to be protective of God. We are afraid when people get that angry with God, afraid they will lose their faith or say something they do not mean. So often we try to keep our words to God nice and sweet. To be sure, manners are important, even when we pray, but no one who has ever loved deeply can be content with mere politeness. The language of love is rightfully thought to be passionate, and it is not always pretty. Jeremiah accused God of seducing him, tricking him, making him look like a fool. Jonah sulked in the face of God's mercy, angry that God was so forgiving. Job raised questions of honor and integrity out of his own anguish, saying even that he wished God had never created him, accusing God of abandoning him. "Sometimes I feel like a motherless child," the Negro spiritual has it, and anyone who has traveled very far in the faith can echo just such sentiments.

Why do you suppose this anguished cry is in the Bible? Would it not have been better to have a hymnbook of psalms that sang happy lyrics of God's goodness and salvation? This psalm is about what it feels like to be crucified.

Jesus once told his disciples that if anyone would come after him, that person must deny herself and take up her cross and follow him. Such a path is not always easy or full of happy rewards. In our culture, we have often thought of the Christian faith as a successful lifestyle, a good thing to do, and one that eventually pays off in material and spiritual ways. And when it does not, or when we are faced with taking up a cross, then we are often baffled. This is what it means to follow Jesus Christ? To live out the lines of this psalm? This feels like abandonment, like being ridiculed, even like being a failure.

"My God, my God, why have you forsaken me?" There is a hidden truth in this psalm we often overlook: Becoming a Christian has a great deal to do with becoming small. Jesus once said that unless we become like a child, we will not enter the kingdom of heaven. Unless a seed falls into the ground and dies, he says, it does not bear fruit. The way we become small is the way of the cross. It is the way of not being self-sufficient; it is the way of many dark nights when you cannot find the way home, when you long for some clearer vision of God. The darkest night of any soul was the night into which Jesus entered on the cross. There he suffered an abandonment that we, by his grace, never have to know. But just there, in his darkest night, we are given a place to go and howl out our anguish and hurt and deepest despair, knowing that he has been there before and is no stranger to such darkness. Here, too, in fact, he leads us. Here, too, he is our good shepherd. And here too, he offers up our hurt and anguish to God.

In saying the book of Psalms displayed the full anatomy of the soul, John Calvin meant that these psalms contain not just the lovely parts of the soul we think are beautiful, but also the hurting parts, the parts we do not want to share with anyone. His point was that God knows all our parts and can bear to hear all our hurts. He has made us, and we are his. Rather than being a denial of faith, our anguished cries are its deepest testimony. "Love hurts," as the song says. It does.

But love also knows from whence cometh our help. The psalmist prays, "Do not be far from me, for trouble is near and there is no one to help." The ultimate calamity, the psalmist suggests, is not death or failure but separation from God. Because God has promised that he will not abandon his own, the psalmist dares to pray this prayer, even dares to throw God's promises back in his face. Do not miss the boldness of this prayer, the daring involved in reminding God of his own promises. That is prayer indeed, prayer at its deepest and most authentic moment, prayer that can join with Job on the ash heap and declare, "For I know that my Redeemer lives, and that at the last he will stand upon the earth; and after my skin has been thus destroyed, then in my flesh I shall see God, whom I shall see on my side, and my eyes shall behold, and not another." To pray like that, even when you do not feel like praying, even when you are dry or weary or despairing—to pray like that is to hang entirely on God's grace. Even in all their anguish, such are the best prayers, the most confident and full of praise. Do not be afraid to dare such prayers, even to pray out your doubts and fears. God has heard such prayers before and knows well the language of the heart and the way we become small enough to enter the kingdom of heaven.

Let us pray: Help me to pray, O Lord. Daily. Help me to pray when I do not much feel like praying or when I doubt or fear. Help me to pray. In Christ's name, I pray. Amen.

NOTES

Psalm 148

Praise the Lord!
Praise the Lord from the heavens; praise him in the
heights!
Praise him, all his angels; praise him, all his host!

Praise him, sun and moon; praise him all you shining
stars!
Praise him, you highest heavens, and you waters
above the heavens!

Let them praise the name of the Lord,
For he commanded and they were created.

He established them forever and ever;
He fixed their bounds, which cannot be passed.

Praise the Lord from the earth, you sea monsters and
all deeps,
Fire and hail, snow and frost, stormy wind
fulfilling his command!

Mountains and all hills, fruit trees and all cedars!
Wild animals and all cattle, creeping things and
flying birds!

Kings of the earth and all peoples,
Princes and all rulers of the earth!
Young men and women alike, old and young together!

Let them praise the name of the Lord,
    For his name alone is exalted;
    His glory is above earth and heaven.
He has raised up a horn for his people, praise for all
    his faithful,
    For the people of Israel who are close to him.
Praise the Lord!

DAY 12

~ ~

PSALM 148

THIS PSALM SEEMS SO SIMPLE: "PRAISE THE LORD!" THAT IS ITS THEME, CONSTANTLY REITERATED THROUGH SEVERAL VERSES. WHAT IS SO WONDERFUL ABOUT SINGING "PRAISE the Lord!"?

Well, look at all the things the psalmist invites to praise the Lord: angels, sun and moon, stars and rain, sea monsters and the depths of oceans, "fire and hail, snow and frost, stormy wind fulfilling his command!" All these things are praising the Lord by their very being. "Mountains and all hills, fruit trees and all cedars!" (As someone who lives in the hill country of Texas, I find it hard to understand how cedars can praise the Lord, but I suppose we should grant the psalmist some poetic license here.) "Wild animals and all cattle, creeping things and flying birds!" All creation, in other words, is invited to enter into the praise of God that never ends, that angels and "creeping things" (bugs? fire ants? centipedes?) instinctively do with their very lives. It is as if the psalmist thinks that this is why the whole universe was created: for the praise of God. For praise, for singing. That is to say, the whole universe is created not just to be consumed, or to be turned into an amusement park, or to be refined into money, but for the praise of its maker. The birds of the air and the lilies of the field seem to know this instinctively. They toil not, neither do they spin. Their flying around, their blooming in the spring, their creeping into a hole are all ways of praising God.

Moreover, this praise happens, the psalmist claims, without our doing anything about it. It just happens. Daily. Flowers praise, lightning sings, thunder rolls. And what are we to do? We are to enter into a praise that began long before we were on the scene. "Kings of the earth and all peoples, princes and all rulers of the earth! Young men and women alike, old and young together! Let them praise the name of the Lord, for his name alone is exalted; his glory is above earth and heaven." We are to become part of the song of creation, to lead it, in fact, as those whom God has especially chosen to tend his garden. We, too, are made, like bees and buffaloes, for a life of praise, a life that finds its center in God and not in ourselves. And when we praise God with our work and our rest, our eating and our sleeping, our worship and our adoration, then we are most who we are, most what we were created to be. That is why we are most human when we worship, when we receive our humanity with the bread and wine that comes from Christ's own hand.

But the truth is we are not bees or buffaloes; we are not birds of the air or lilies of the field. We do not praise God with our very being. We have to think about it, work at it, be reminded of it. Sometimes it is very hard for us to praise God. We do not feel like it, or we are tired or angry or lonely. Moreover, praising God often does not seem like much of a gift to us. Rather, it seems a chore, something we have to work at. We long for moments when praise becomes a spontaneous thing, when our hearts are lifted up and we burst into song. But such moments, although hardly unknown, do not characterize our daily lives. We find praise difficult.

Which is one reason we go to worship, to remember the gift, to be reminded of the blessings of praise, to be helped and encouraged by others who praise. We forget. And so we must be taught the songs again and again and listen to the music all over again. We have to learn to enter into creation's praise, to participate in the praise we have not made but can only receive. That is why worship is rather like learning to speak a new language. We must be immersed in it. We are drilled with responsive readings, scripture passages, hymns of praise, until, slowly, we can speak the language by heart. Then praise, rather than seeming a chore or something we do, becomes something we enter into, something in which we participate, something that we miss when we fail to sing and give thanks.

My mother taught me to pray, just as she taught me to worship. She would line out the hymns with her finger, and I would follow along. She taught me to sing in parts, to learn the rhythm of worship, the various responses and prayers. As the one who cradled me in her arms and first spoke to me, she helped me learn the language of worship, to miss it when it was not spoken, to cultivate the gift of worship that never ceases, the praise that never ends.

The psalmist thinks that we cannot praise God alone but only in the company of God's people, the church. There, work and worship become a gift; there, creation and covenant become one; there, we, for a moment, become like the birds of the air and the lilies of the field, and our lives are "lost in wonder, love, and praise." Praise the Lord!

Let us pray: Teach me the songs of praise, O Lord, that I might ever sing and be glad. Lead me to your people, I pray, that I might ever join in the praise that is everlasting. Show me the daily beauty of sky and wind, of bird and flower, that I might join with them in finding the music to praise the Lord. In Christ's name I pray. Amen.

NOTES

Psalm 73

*Truly God is good to the upright, to those who are
pure in heart.
But as for me, my feet had almost stumbled; my steps
had nearly slipped.
For I was envious of the arrogant; I saw the
prosperity of the wicked.*

*For they have no pain; their bodies are sound and
sleek.
They are not in trouble as others are; they are not
plagued like other people.
Therefore pride is their necklace; violence covers them
like a garment.
Their eyes swell out with fatness; their hearts
overflow with follies.
They scoff and speak with malice; loftily they
threaten oppression.
They set their mouths against heaven, and their
tongues range over the earth.*

*Therefore the people turn and praise them, and find
no fault in them.
And they say, "How can God know? Is there
knowledge in the Most High?"
Such are the wicked; always at ease, they increase in
riches.
All in vain I have kept my heart clean and washed
my hands in innocence.*

For all day long I have been plagued, and am
    punished every morning.

If I had said, "I will talk on in this way,"
I would have been untrue to the circle of your
    children.
But when I thought how to understand this, it
    seemed to me a wearisome task,
Until I went into the sanctuary of God; then I
    perceived their end.
Truly you set them in slippery places; you make them
    fall to ruin.
How they are destroyed in a moment, swept away
    utterly by terrors!
They are like a dream when one awakes; on awaking
    you despise their phantoms.

When my soul was embittered, when I was pricked in
    heart,
I was stupid and ignorant; I was like a brute beast
    toward you.
Nevertheless, I am continually with you; you hold
    my right hand.
You guide me with your counsel, and afterward you
    will receive me with honor.
Whom have I in heaven but you?
And there is nothing on earth that I desire other
    than you.

My flesh and my heart may fail,
But God is the strength of my heart and my portion
   forever.

Indeed, those who are far from you will perish;
You put an end to those who are false to you.
But for me it is good to be near God;
I have made the Lord God my refuge, to tell of all
    your works.

DAY 13

—•—

PSALM 73

ONE OF THE THINGS THAT TROUBLED THIS PSALMIST WAS THE SIMPLE FACT THAT THOSE WHO ARE GOOD ARE NOT ALWAYS REWARDED FOR BEING GOOD, AND EVEN WORSE, those who do evil often prosper. This is troubling. It is not supposed to be like that. It is supposed to be more straight-forward: Do good and you will prosper; do evil and you will only hurt yourself.

When I was in the eighth grade, I had a hard time with algebra. No, that is not true; I hated algebra and was almost flunking. What made things worse was that my two older sisters were math whizzes, and my father loved math and could not understand why I could not get it. But I could not. And I grew more and more angry and frustrated. My math teacher, an ancient but energetic little woman, used to warn us before every test not to cheat: "You'll only be hurting yourselves," she would say. I used to wonder about that. In fact, I did not cheat because it would not have done me any good. I did not know enough algebra to know how to cheat! Believe me, I was a terrible math student. Still, I wondered if what she said were true. I had no plans to be a math major, much less to run a nuclear submarine. I was going to try to find a field of work as far away from num-bers as I possibly could. So how could I hurt myself if I cheated? No one else would know, and as long as I never gave myself out as a math whiz, I would not ever be called on to give an account of my "knowledge." Besides, I knew folks who cheated, and they seemed to be doing pretty well. They were not geniuses, but they were doing better than I was. Moreover, their fathers never asked them why they did not "get it." No, in truth, they prospered.

"For I was envious of the arrogant; I saw the prosperity of the wicked." The psalmist may not have been in my math class, but he noticed that the world "ain't the way it's supposed to be." He envies those who have got ahead without getting caught. "For they have no pain; their bodies are sound and sleek. They are not in trouble as others are; they are not plagued like other people. . . . Therefore the people turn and praise them, and find no fault in them. And they say, 'How can God know? Is there knowledge in the Most High?'"

If God knows the hearts of his children, why are the evil not zapped when they do evil? After awhile, people start laughing at God. "What does he know?" they ask. "I cheated and got away with it. I stole and was never caught. God is an old fool. You can steal him blind." "Such are the wicked; always at ease, they increase in riches. All in vain I have kept my heart clean and washed my hands in innocence." All in vain have I struggled to lead a good life.

Hard to understand that this is the way the world operates. An old poem cynically captures the psalmist's complaints well:

> The rain it raineth all around,
> On the just and unjust fella;
> But mostly on the just, because
> The unjust has stolen the just's umbrella.

"But when I thought how to understand this, it seemed to me a wearisome task, until I went into the sanctuary of God; then I perceived their end. Truly you set them in slippery places; you make them fall to ruin. How they are destroyed in a moment, swept away utterly by terrors!"

My Sunday School class has been reading *Macbeth,* a play
you may have already read. In that play, Macbeth claws his
way to the top, even killing his lord and king to get there,
and no one but he and his wife know how black are his
crimes. He has succeeded. And he becomes king of Scot-
land. There is only one problem: he cannot sleep at night.
Slowly, in a terrifying way, he begins to crumble, losing
everything, but most especially losing his own soul. He
loses himself.

There are worse things than not getting what you want;
there are even worse things than being a poor algebra student, as I certainly was. The worst thing might indeed be
getting exactly what you want but losing your own soul. You
might succeed only to lead a silly or trivial life, unable to
give much or believe in much or hope in much. When the
psalmist went into the sanctuary, there he saw God's economy: not the economy of success, but the economy of
grace, the working out of integrity and love and commitment in an honorable life. It may not look like much to
some. Indeed, it may look like a lower grade than you would
have wanted, or a disappointment you have to live with, or
a slow and steady plodding to the finish. Indeed, it may
some day look like a cross. But in the economy of grace,
even the cross becomes a gift. It teaches us that we live not
by what we give ourselves but by what we receive from
God's own hand. That is what is so hard to believe: God is
shaping you through his gifts so that you become a gift yourself. "You guide me with your counsel, and afterward you
will receive me with honor. Whom have I in heaven but you?
And there is nothing on earth that I desire other than you."
It is not that "you only hurt yourself." In truth, often you do
not. It is that you miss the gift. You lose heart. You trust only
in what you can achieve yourself.

The way is not easy; the Christian faith is hard. That is
why its symbol is the cross. But finally, it is not even hard:

It is impossible. That is why the cross is a symbol of grace. It takes a miracle for us to become followers of Jesus Christ. The tragedy is not that we fail in our efforts; the tragedy is that we overlook the gift of the cross, that we fail to celebrate or sing of God's grace to us in Jesus Christ. The psalmist did not get things straightened out until he went to church and worshiped. Then he could let his bitterness go and give up comparing himself with others and receive himself instead from God's own hands.

God is good, and he is no fool. The evil have their reward, no small part of which is the hell of having to live with the gifts that they give themselves, condemned to making do with their "success." What the psalmist discovered is the better gift of being surprised by grace, of not being ashamed of being in need, of learning the joy of asking. Just so are we brought closer to God and his gifts; just so do we become like children who ask; just so do we glimpse something of the kingdom of heaven. "My heart and my flesh may fail, but God is the strength of my heart and my portion forever."

Let us pray: Grant me contentment, Lord. Not self-satisfaction, not laziness, but simple contentment: a happiness that I am your child and you are my heavenly Father. Keep me from comparing myself with others, and give me the grace to find in the cross of Jesus Christ the gift of my own life that comes from your hands. In the name of Jesus Christ, I pray. Amen.

NOTES

Psalm 121

I lift up my eyes to the hills—from where will my
    help come?
My help comes from the Lord, who made heaven and
    earth.

He will not let your foot be moved; he who keeps you
    will not slumber.
He who keeps Israel will neither slumber nor sleep.

The Lord is your keeper; the Lord is your shade at
    your right hand.
The sun shall not strike you by day, nor the moon by
    night.

The Lord will keep you from all evil; he will keep
    your life.
The Lord will keep your going out and your
    coming in
    From this time on and forevermore.

DAY 14

PSALM 121

T HIS IS A FAVORITE PSALM OF THOSE OF US WHO LIVE IN THE HILL COUNTRY. IT BEGINS: "I LIFT UP MY EYES TO THE HILLS—FROM WHERE DOES MY HELP COME?" WE CAN relate to that. Each morning when I go for a walk with my dogs, we head south down our street, and I can look into the far distance and see across the Guadalupe River valley to the hills beyond. It is a lovely sight. "I lift up my eyes to the hills—from where does my help come?"

The psalmist, however, did not look to the hills just for the aesthetic satisfaction they provided. In his day, the hills were thought of as the place where gods lived. The tops of mountains were thought to be holy places. It was on top of Mount Sinai that Moses received the Ten Commandments from God. Maybe, some thought, the hills were magic places, places like Mount Olympus in Greece where gods and goddesses cavorted and from whence they occasionally descended to intervene in the affairs of mortals. Maybe, to carry this thought further, we should look to the hills for help; maybe we should pray to them as "holy places." "I lift up my eyes to the hills" the psalmist asks, "from where does my help come?"

And he answers his own question: "My help comes from the Lord who made heaven and earth." In other words, my help comes not from the hills, as mighty and beautiful as they are; my help comes from the one who made the hills, the one "who made heaven and earth." The hills do not protect you when you stumble or fall, but "He will not let your foot be moved." He watches over you when you are unable to watch over yourself; that is how he has watched over his own people Israel. "Behold, he who keeps Israel will neither slumber nor sleep."

The psalmist concludes by telling us that as the one who watches over Israel, the Lord is our keeper, the one who keeps our life in the strength of his own hands. "The Lord will keep you from all evil; he will keep your life. The Lord will keep your going out and your coming in from this time on and forevermore."

Maybe it does not seem like good news to you to learn that you have a keeper. It almost implies that you live in a zoo. There are times when I feel as if I live in a zoo, but, if I did, I would not want to be reminded of it or reminded that I have a keeper. But the psalmist is telling us that in this crazy world in which we live, we have someone who cares for us, who does not sleep when we do, who gives us rest, who watches over us when we lose sight of ourselves. In his hands are all our days. This God even has "the little bitty baby in his hands." He does, just as he has you and me. The psalmist found comfort in that. For one thing, he no longer had to pretend to be God all the time, trying to stay awake and keep himself and others straight. He could rather be simply human. He could entrust his life into God's hands and let God be God. God can do that, and in doing that, God will "keep me." And I will be free to rejoice in my full humanity: to work and sleep and study and worship and share and hope. God, after all, is in control. He is my help.

There is no better news than that. And there are times when we become more aware of this grace than we usually are. When we are oppressed on every side, when life in this zoo becomes more than we can handle, then we can be grateful that we have a "keeper" who has not fallen asleep on the job and who will take care of us.

A friend of mine was having a picnic with her pastor a long time ago. It started to rain and here in the hill country a little rain can make a creek rise very rapidly. My friend's children were on the other side of the creek and would be unable to cross over once the creek rose. My friend asked her pastor, "What are we going to do? My children will not be able to get across the creek." And her pastor (Dick Ryan, a former pastor of this church) told her, "Well, I don't know what we will do, but I know this: God is Lord on both sides of that creek."

I have often thought about that story: "God is Lord on both sides of that creek." He is, and he is watching over you. "The Lord will keep your going out and your coming in from this time forth and forevermore."

Let us pray: Thank you, Lord, for keeping me; for watching over me through the night and at other times when I am quite unable to watch over myself. Help me to be glad that I do have a keeper, and in that keeper's care, nothing can separate me from his love. Thank you for freeing me from worrying all the time about myself, or even about my salvation, and for giving me the liberty to think of others, to see the needs of others, above all, to serve Jesus Christ and tell of his goodness and enjoy his grace. I make my prayer in his name. Amen.

Psalm 46

God is our refuge and strength, a very present help in
* trouble.*
Therefore we will not fear, though the earth should
* change,*
* Though the mountains shake in the heart of the*
* sea;*
Though its waters roar and foam,
* Though the mountains tremble with its tumult.*

There is a river whose streams make glad the city of
* God,*
* The holy habitation of the Most High.*
God is in the midst of the city; it shall not be moved;
God will help it when the morning dawns.
The nations are in an uproar, the kingdoms totter;
* He utters his voice, the earth melts.*
The Lord of hosts is with us; the God of Jacob is our
* refuge.*

Come, behold the works of the Lord;
* See what desolations he has brought on the earth.*
He makes wars cease to the end of the earth;
* He breaks the bow, and shatters the spear; he*
* burns the shields with fire.*
"Be still, and know that I am God!
* I am exalted among the nations, I am exalted in*
* the earth."*
The Lord of hosts is with us; the God of Jacob is our
* refuge.*

DAY 15

———

PSALM 46

IN READING THESE PSALMS, ARE YOU EVER STRUCK BY THE FACT THAT SO OFTEN THE PSALMIST APPEARS TO BE IN TROUBLE? IT SEEMS TO ME THAT A NUMBER OF THESE PSALMS WERE WRITTEN by people who were desperate, who needed big-time help. Psalm 46 is such a psalm: "God is our refuge and strength, a very present help in time of trouble."

It is hard to escape the conclusion that the book of Psalms was written by people who had trouble, whose lives were often chaotic, who sensed that they were in over their heads. You do not really need prayer if life has no real challenges, if you never incur any real enemies, if your heart has never been broken. Indeed, if all we have to worry about is how to manage our affluence, then prayer must seem to us to be either silly or hypocritical.

That is why the Psalms so often bring us back to reality. Yesterday, I visited with a man in the hospital who has liver cancer and is dying. The doctors had just left his room, having told him that he was going to be released to his home to be put under hospice care. Nothing else could be done. He was angry and frightened and somewhat stunned. I listened to him vent some of his anger and finally offered to pray with him. "What good will that do?" he asked me. "I don't know," I replied, "but you've got trouble, and when I have trouble I take it to God. He deals with trouble."

That is how the psalmist begins. He reminds us that "God is our refuge and strength, a very present help in time of trouble." I suppose if we had no needs and could just sail through life, we might never discover our need of God. In any case, the psalmist does not think that God will snap his fingers and make the trouble go away. But he does believe that in the midst of trouble, God is there and does not abandon him. "Therefore," he writes, "we will not fear though the earth should change, though the mountains shake in the heart of the sea. . . . The nations are in an uproar, the kingdoms totter; he utters his voice, the earth melts. The Lord of hosts is with us; the God of Jacob is our refuge."

How does God help? Like a mother who quiets a child at her breast, God comforts us. He brings peace. He "makes wars cease to the end of the earth; he breaks the bow, and shatters the spear; he burns the chariots with fire." He takes all the instruments of war, some of which we use against others, some of which we find in the battles going on in our own hearts, and he makes peace.

"Be still, and know that I am God!"

One of the reasons we find prayer difficult, I think, is because it is so constantly embarrassing to us. It reminds us of our needs, of our helplessness, of our troubles. We would like to be like the folks we dream about who have no troubles, who have everything under control. Prayer is a confession that we are not in control, not even in control of our own lives. We need help. Just so, however, prayer is a confession that we are not called to the business of managing small things, but living courageously in the face of big things, even overwhelming things. We may not be in control, but life is not out of control for God is Lord. "He is our refuge and strength." Because he is our "very present help in time of trouble," we can live courageously. We can pray as big-hearted people, people can encompass suffering and heartbreak and loss and can still hope. People who pray like that endure. They understand something of the wonderful gift of "being still" and knowing that God is Lord. Sometimes that is enough: just being still and resting in God's presence. How much time do we devote to watching television, or distracting ourselves with some other entertainment? A good deal, I suspect, and not all such time is wasted. But when was the last time we wasted some time with God? Prayer, like worship itself, is the gift of wasting time with God, the God who has all the time in the world for us. It is a gift to be still.

Let us pray: Our Father, I would like to waste some time with you this day: to receive your gifts, to give thanks for the life you have shared with me, to follow Jesus Christ. You are my refuge and strength and will always be a very present help in time of trouble. Help me never to be afraid to ask, never to be ashamed of the hard work of praying. I pray this in the name of Jesus Christ. Amen.

Psalm 84

How lovely is your dwelling place, O Lord of hosts!
My soul longs, indeed it faints for the courts of the Lord;
 My heart and my flesh sing for joy to the living God.

Even the sparrow finds a home, and the swallow a
 nest for herself,
 Where she may lay her young, at your altars, O
 Lord of hosts,
 My king and my God.
Happy are those who live in your house, ever singing
 your praise.

Happy are those whose strength is in you,
 In whose heart are the highways to Zion.
As they go through the valley of Baca they make it a
 place of springs;
 The early rain also covers it with pools.
They go from strength to strength; the God of gods
 will be seen in Zion.

O Lord God of hosts, hear my prayer; give ear, O God
 of Jacob!

Behold our shield, O God; look on the face of your
 anointed.

For a day in your courts is better than a thousand
 elsewhere.
I would rather be a doorkeeper in the house of my God
 Than live in the tents of wickedness.

---

*For the Lord God is a sun and shield; he bestows
  favor and honor.*
*No good thing does the Lord withhold from those
  who walk uprightly.*
O Lord of hosts, happy is everyone who trusts in you.

DAY 16

⌒ ⌒

"HOW LOVELY IS YOUR DWELLING PLACE, O LORD OF HOSTS! MY SOUL LONGS, INDEED IT FAINTS FOR THE COURTS OF THE LORD; MY HEART AND FLESH SING FOR JOY TO THE living God."

This psalm is about a person who loves to worship, a person whose soul is fed in worship, a person who thinks of worship as her home. She knows the songs, she knows the sanctuary, the building, the windows, the music, the words. And she feels at home there. "Even the sparrow finds a home, and the swallow a nest for herself, where she may lay her young, at your altars, O Lord of hosts, my King and my God." Like a bird whose nest is under the eaves of the church, this psalmist nests in the sanctuary and there raises her young so that they too might learn to sing praise to the Lord of hosts.

"Happy are those who live in your house, ever singing your praise." I can remember worshiping with my mother when I was a child. In addition to lining out the hymns for me and helping me through the various parts of the liturgy, she taught me how to worship. I do not mean that she taught me when to stand up or sit down, when to sing or be quiet, although she did teach me these things, too. I mean she taught me the attitude of worship: how to drink in the silence, how to listen so hard my ears hurt, how to wait on God's word and allow that word to shape my response. My mother did not like worship in which we always have the first word and send God on our little errands. She listened and allowed the story of God's grace to shape her desires and hopes and joys.

Once during a final hymn, I saw my mother weeping. I asked her why she was crying; had I done something wrong? She smiled at me and said, "I'm just so happy." At the time I did not know how one could be so happy as to weep. Now I do. So did the psalmist. Sometimes the goodness of God to us in Jesus Christ just overwhelms. And we should not be ashamed to admit it. "Happy are those who live in your house, ever singing your praise."

Such happiness is the result of God's word shaping our lives. That is what happens when we "eat" God's word. When we eat the bread and wine, the bread and wine are not transformed so much as we are who receive it as the body and blood of Jesus Christ. Similarly, when we eat God's word of scripture, it has a way of changing our lives, of making us different. "As they go through the valley of Baca they make it a place of springs." Baca was a dry place, a hard place. The psalmist says that those who worship in God's house are a blessing to the world; they are like spring rains in West Texas. They create, in the dry land, pools of water for thirsty creatures to drink. This is a wonderful image, and true to life, I believe. There are people who have been for me a "pool of water." My mother was one. Her faith was a pool to which I returned to drink again and again. Worship regularly creates such "pools of water" in a dry land for thirsty people.

The psalmist concludes with the words: "For a day in your courts is better than a thousand elsewhere. I would rather be a doorkeeper in the house of my God than live in the tents of wickedness."

Just as the psalms often speak of being in trouble, so do they just as often tell us that it is impossible to believe in this God in isolation from other believers. The reason a day in

God's house is better than a thousand elsewhere is that in that house we are grafted into a community of faith and are given a story that sustains our lives. It is a great myth of the modern world (and the ancient world, for that matter) that we do not need one another or the community of faith to be faithful. In part to puncture such a myth, Ralph Wood recalled the story of Saint Augustine after he embraced the Christian faith but before he decided to be baptized as a publicly avowed believer. Augustine reflected on an earlier discussion that took place between two of his friends, Victorinus and Simplicianus. Victorinus had read the Bible and studied Christian theology, yet Simplicianus contended that Victorinus would not really be a believer until he was received into the church of Jesus Christ. "Then do walls make Christians?" Victorinus asked impatiently. For many in our culture today, the answer is a clear and impassioned No. "You can become a Christian by going to church," Garrison Keillor is reported to have said, "about as easily as you can become a car by sleeping in a garage."[6] Yet I wonder. In any case, Augustine would have disagreed with Keillor, and he would have disagreed not because he thought the church was without blemish but because he believed that Christians are made by being engrafted into Israel's story, by becoming part of the body of Christ, the church. There we are formed by worshiping communities into something more than ourselves and our own choices. There we are enabled to "put on Christ" and live happily as his servants in the world.[7] I would rather be a doorkeeper in such a house than live "freely" in a world that thinks that becoming a Christian is a matter of self-invention.

6. As cited in Barbara Brown Taylor's article "Leaving the Church," *The Christian Century*, 16–23 June, 1999, 655.
7. From "Staying in the Church," an unpublished article by Ralph C. Wood, accompanying a letter dated 13 August, 1999, to Thomas W. Currie III.

Let us pray: Grant me, O Lord, the gift of worship, the gift of praise, the gift of "putting on Christ." That is what I ask. Help me to become like a pool of water from which the thirsty can drink and be refreshed. So may my life drink from the stream of living water that is Jesus Christ. In his name, I offer this prayer. Amen.

Psalm 8

O Lord, our Sovereign, how majestic is your name in
all the earth!

You have set your glory above the heavens.
Out of the mouths of babes and infants you have
founded a bulwark
Because of your foes, to silence the enemy and the
avenger.

When I look at your heavens, the work of your fingers,
The moon and the stars that you have established;
What are human beings that you are mindful of
them,
Mortals that you care for them?

Yet you have made them a little lower than God,
And crowned them with glory and honor.
You have given them dominion over the works of your
hands;
You have put all things under their feet,
All sheep and oxen, and also the beasts of the
field,
The birds of the air, and the fish of the sea,
Whatever passes along the paths of the seas.

O Lord, our Sovereign, how majestic is your name in
all the earth!

DAY 17

---◆◆---

PSALM 8

WHEN I WAS A LITTLE BOY, A FRIEND WHO LIVED DOWN THE STREET INVITED ME TO SPEND THE NIGHT WITH HIM, SLEEPING IN A PUP TENT IN HIS BACKYARD. THIS seemed to me to be a great adventure, and I was glad when my mother said that I could go. We set up the tent, as I recall, in striking distance of his back porch so that if anything happened, we could beat a hasty retreat into his house. Also, his mother's kitchen was just inside the back porch, and we thought we might sneak in and grab some chocolate chip cookies if we got hungry. But what I remember most about that night was lying down with my head outside the tent flap and looking up at the stars. In the city, the lights are so bright you do not usually see too many stars, but we lived at the edge of town and so could still see a good many. They were like mosquitoes buzzing about my head. All of a sudden, I seemed very small. Have you ever had that experience? You look into the infinite vastness of space, and you begin to sense how small you are. Who am I? What am I doing here, a little speck of a person on a little speck of a planet, looking into the immensity of stars and dust and empty space? I remember feeling almost lonely at that moment, sensing that I was alone in the universe.

The psalmist asks much the same questions when he looks up at the sky: "When I look at your heavens, the work of your fingers, the moon and the stars that you have established;

what are human beings that you are mindful of them, mortals that you care for them?" Who are we to be so small?

But then he answers his own question. In praising God, he says: "Yet you have made them a little lower than God, and crowned them with glory and honor." In the scheme of creation, we are given a place. We may think we are small, given the vastness of space, but in our world we are not small. We, in fact, have what the psalmist calls "dominion" over creation. That is, we are stewards of this earth; we have power over creation but power that is responsible to another. We can abuse and destroy what God has made or cultivate its fruitfulness and live as if what God has made is our "home." The psalmist knows that human beings have enormous powers that cannot be wished away. We are almost godlike in what we can do: invent computers, fly to the moon, perform heart surgery, heal diseases. In many ways, we seem to be at the center of creation. "What are human beings that you are mindful of them?" Strangely, the psalmist seems to think that human beings are a fascinating part of creation, the "apple" of God's eye, the most awesome part of creation itself.

But then he ends, not with praise of human beings, but with the praise of God: "O Lord, our Sovereign, how majestic is your name in all the earth!" It is God who has made us and not we ourselves, and if we have been given an important role to play in creation, it is because God has given us that role.

It is fashionable, given the various environmental crises, to bewail the presence of human beings on the earth. Our national parks would be so lovely, we are often told, if there were no people there. Overcoming the threat that human beings represent to the environment often seems such a massive task that we come to despair, even hate our own humanity. But this psalmist does not permit himself such a luxury, anymore than he thinks that human beings can thwart the goodness of God's creation. Finally, it is the Lord who is sovereign, not human beings. We can truly exercise dominion only by learning to praise the Lord of all creation.

Karl Barth suggested that this psalm is really not even about us in the first place. What this psalm is really about is Jesus Christ, the true human being. (The author of Hebrews agrees. You might want to look at Heb. 2:5–9.) Jesus is that human being who is at the center of creation, who exercises dominion over the creatures through his cross. If we want to find out what it is to be a human being, we must first look at him. We spend a lifetime trying to figure ourselves out and to find our place in the world. Often we think we can do so only by looking at ourselves. It is easy to think we must be important because we can do so many technologically powerful things. Our culture, as has often been pointed out, is technologically rich but spiritually poor. As Harry Emerson Fosdick's hymn has it, we are "rich in things and poor in soul."[8] When we define ourselves in terms of all the things we can do or all the possessions we have amassed, we grow more and more confused as to our own identity. It is as if we were at a carnival and were looking at a mirror in a funhouse: The culture bends and distorts us in so many ways. But when we discern our image in Jesus Christ, then in him our identity becomes clear. He is the one who possesses dominion, who is crowned with glory and honor, whom all of creation serves. We enter into his stewardship as we serve him, just as we become truly persons as we receive our humanity from him. That is how we learn to sing, "O Lord, our Sovereign, how majestic is your name in all the earth!"

Let us pray: Thank you, Lord, for all you have created. Thank you for creating birds and rocks, trees and oceans,

8. Harry Emerson Fosdick, "God of Grace and God of Glory," in *The Presbyterian Hymnal* (Louisville: Presbyterian Church USA, 1993) #420, v. 3.

but thank you also for creating me. Help me not to abuse what you have created or belittle it, but to give thanks and to offer myself in your service. The sea is wide, O Lord, and my little boat is so small. Be with me throughout this day, and, at the end of this day, grant me safe harbor in your love. In Jesus Christ's name, I pray. Amen.

NOTES

Psalm 90

Lord, you have been our dwelling place in all
    generations.
Before the mountains were brought forth,
    Or ever you had formed the earth and the world,
    From everlasting to everlasting you are God.

You turn us back to dust, and say, "Turn back, you
    mortals."
For a thousand years in your sight are like yesterday
    when it is past,
    Or like a watch in the night.

You sweep them away; they are like a dream,
    Like grass that is renewed in the morning;
    In the morning it flourishes and is renewed;
    In the evening it fades and withers.

For we are consumed by your anger;
    By your wrath we are overwhelmed.
You have set our iniquities before you,
    Our secret sins in the light of your countenance.

For all our days pass away under your wrath;
    Our years come to an end like a sigh.
The days of our life are seventy years, or perhaps
    eighty, if we are strong;
    Even then their span is only toil and trouble.
    They are soon gone, and we fly away.

Who considers the power of your anger?
    Your wrath is as great as the fear that is due you.
So teach us to count our days that we may gain a
    wise heart.

Turn, O Lord! How long?
    Have compassion on your servants!
Satisfy us in the morning with your steadfast love,
    So that we may rejoice and be glad all our days.
Make us glad as many days as you have afflicted us,
    And as many years as we have seen evil.
Let your work be manifest to your servants,
    And your glorious power to their children.
Let the favor of the Lord our God be upon us,
    And prosper for us the work of our hands—
O prosper the work of our hands!

DAY 18

—◆◆—

PSALM 90

"LORD, YOU HAVE BEEN OUR DWELLING PLACE IN ALL GENERATIONS." ONE OF THE GREATEST TEMPTATIONS A CHRISTIAN MUST FACE IS THE TEMPTATION TO BELIEVE THAT the faith begins with "me." Unless I affirm it as true, it is not true, or so we are tempted to think. That is the American way. Faith is something I verify and confirm, something I choose and make real. But this psalmist would disagree. He knows that God has been on the scene long before he was born. He knows that the faith has been confessed by his family for generations and that he has received this faith from their hands along with their love. He could no more confess this faith by himself than he could be a brother or a son or a father by himself. For him to say "I believe" means for him to stand in relationship with others, with Israel, with God. That is what it is to have faith: not to think up something religious but to be joined to that family of folk whose life has been narrated by this story of faith. "Lord, you are the beginning of our story and the end; you are the narrative whose plot makes sense of our lives. Lord, you have been our dwelling place in all generations."

God is our beginning. God is before us. "Before the mountains were brought forth, or ever you had formed the earth and the world, from everlasting to everlasting you are God." Throughout the history of the church, when folk have reflected on the faith, they have tended to place great emphasis on the priority of God. We pray only in answer to what God has spoken first. Our first words are always "Thank you," because they do not come first. God's grace has preceded them, evoked them. God is first, and to believe in God is to receive my life from his hands; it is to understand my whole life as an answer to God's word of grace. That is why so much of the Christian life is nothing more than learning to say "Thank you."

But just as we first learn to say "Thank you," the second thing we learn to say is "Help!" "The days of our life are seventy years, or perhaps eighty, if we are strong; even then their span is only toil and trouble; they are soon gone, and we fly away. . . . So teach us to count our days that we may gain a wise heart."

Counting our days is the way to do the arithmetic of grace, the way we acknowledge that "our help is in the name of the Lord." When all our days seem numbered and we have grown weary and weak, even then we know we are in God's good care. We live toward God. God is our end. What people thought in the medieval period is true: We are on a pilgrimage. This pilgrimage is not an endless road with option after meaningless option, none of which leads anywhere. No, we are not tourists but pilgrims. We are on a journey that leads to God. To number our days is simply to rejoice in that fact, to celebrate that one in whose hands are all our days and who knows us better than we know ourselves. Sometimes this pilgrimage seems long and hard, sometimes we lose our way badly. But the one who teaches us to number our days is the one who does not ever let us go. He will "make us glad as many days" as we are afflicted. He never loses us.

That is why the psalmist ends with a prayer that God will help him surround the next generation with the words and songs of faith that have nourished him. That is why, as odd as this may strike you, I am writing this little book of prayers and meditations for you. My father sent me off to college with a similar book of prayers and meditations, and they surrounded me with the words of "thank you" and "help," words of hope and praise. Just so is God's work made "manifest" to his servants and his "glorious power to their children." (v. 16) And just so, does praying cease to be a duty and come to resemble something more like a song. In that singing, the lonely pilgrim who is struggling to put one foot in front of the other discovers that she is in the midst of a happy company of good companions walking alongside her, all going in the same direction. "Let the favor of the Lord our God be upon us, and prosper for us the work of our hands—O prosper the work of our hands!"

Let us pray: Keep me on the way, O Lord. Make me mindful that I do not walk alone, any more than I pray alone, but am surrounded by your Holy Spirit and pray words that are lifted up to heaven by your Son, Jesus Christ, who has given me an entire company of saints to love and to learn from. Help me not to despise or hold that company in contempt but to join with them, in following Jesus Christ. In his name, I pray. Amen.

NOTES

Psalm 91

You who live in the shelter of the Most High,
  Who abide in the shadow of the Almighty,
Will say to the Lord, "My refuge and my fortress; my
  God, in whom I trust."
For he will deliver you from the snare of the fowler
  And from the deadly pestilence;
He will cover you with his pinions, and under his
  wings you will find refuge;
  His faithfulness is a shield and buckler.
You will not fear the terror of the night, or the arrow
  that flies by day,
  Or the pestilence that stalks in darkness,
  Or the destruction that wastes at noonday.

A thousand may fall at your side, ten thousand at
  your right hand,
  But it will not come near you.
You will only look with your eyes and see the
  punishment of the wicked.

Because you have made the Lord your refuge,
  The Most High your dwelling place,
  No evil shall befall you, no scourge come near
  your tent.

For he will command his angels concerning you to
  guard you in all your ways.
On their hands they will bear you up,
  So that you will not dash your foot against a
  stone.

You will tread on the lion and the adder,
  The young lion and the serpent you will trample
  under foot.

Those who love me, I will deliver;
  I will protect those who know my name.
When they call to me, I will answer them;
  I will be with them in trouble,
  I will rescue them and honor them.
With long life I will satisfy them, and show them my
  salvation.

DAY 19

—◆——◆—

PSALM 91

I HAVE ALWAYS THOUGHT THAT PSALMS 90 AND 91 WERE MEANT TO BE READ TOGETHER AND THAT IT IS NO ACCIDENT THAT ONE FOLLOWS THE OTHER. PSALM 90 CONTRASTS THE everlastingness of God with our brief span of years on earth. We are like grass, "renewed in the morning," but in the evening, faded and withered. On the other hand, a thousand years for God are "like yesterday when it is past, or like a watch in the night." Psalm 90 emphasizes the distance between the Holy God who has created us and our own fragile and temporal life as creatures.

Psalm 91, however, tells us of God's closeness to us. "You who live in the shelter of the Most High, who abide in the shadow of the Almighty, will say to the Lord, 'My refuge and my fortress, my God in whom I trust.' For he will deliver you from the snare of the fowler and from the deadly pestilence." He is as close to you as a mother eagle is to her eaglets: "He will cover you with his pinions, and under his wings you will find refuge." With such protection, we need not fear: "You will not fear the terror of the night, or the arrow that flies by day, or the pestilence that stalks in darkness, or the destruction that wastes at noonday."

This psalm assumes that we have reason to be afraid. There are things "out there" that are scary, the psalmist thinks. He does not identify them all, but he speaks of the

"terror of the night," "the arrow that flies by day," "the pestilence that stalks in darkness," and the "destruction that
wastes at noonday." The terror of the night? What could that
be? A number of things, I suppose, but I wonder if it might
not simply be loneliness. I do not mean just the loneliness
that feels friendless or forlorn, but a deeper loneliness that
feels abandoned by God. Someone once said that at 3 o'clock
in the morning, we are all atheists. What he meant is that at
that hour we have a hard time sensing God's presence. I have
been with alcoholics at that hour and have sometimes felt
that if they could just make it to sunrise, they would be all
right. They felt so alone in the darkness. What a gift not to
feel the terror of the night, to be able to be like a child and
go to sleep, trusting that God would watch over us.

At the very end of Harper Lee's *To Kill a Mockingbird*, she
has Scout tell of how her father, Atticus, tucked her into bed
following the "terror of the night" that befell her and Jem as
they came back from the Halloween program at the school.
After he left her room, "He turned out the light and went
into Jem's room. He would be there all night, and he would
be there when Jem waked up in the morning."[9] So does our
heavenly Father watch over us all night and greet us fresh
with his grace in the morning.

"The arrow that flies by day" is also something the
psalmist fears. What could that be? Tests, exams, assign-
ments, work? All of that has somehow to be negotiated. We
can dodge some arrows more easily than others, but all of
them have to be turned or warded off. They "test" us, and if
we do not have the strength or the protection or the agility
to deal with them, then one of them might well wound us.
God, the psalmist insists, is our "shield," the source of our
agility and spirit. He goes into battle with us and does not

9. Harper Lee, *To Kill a Mockingbird* (New York: Warner Books, 1982), 284.

let those arrows penetrate our flesh. Indeed, he helps us overcome every threat, not by some magic charm but by his hope-inducing presence, by his discipline-making love, by his courage-creating faith. Yes, he is with us in the midst of the arrows that come our way daily.

"The pestilence that stalks in darkness"? What is that? Pestilence is an illness, a contagious sickness that can quickly lead to death. Perhaps that is all the psalmist has in mind. God is our healer and protector. But I wonder whether the psalmist does not also think of pestilence as the kind of pollution we have to live with, the pollution that poisons our spirits and invites us to trivialize our lives by "amusing ourselves to death."[10] I am a card-carrying member of the "me generation," so that I know how easy it is to come down with such a pestilential illness, an illness that invites me to think that I am the center of the world. In some ways, that must be what hell is like. When I am at the center of the world, my world has grown very small indeed. We do well to fear the "pestilence that stalks in darkness." It leads to what Martin Luther called "the heart curved in on itself," the hell in which we are unable to forget ourselves. What a gift to have this God who opens us up like a flower to receive the sunshine and rain of his grace.

"The destruction that wastes at noonday"? This too sounds like a battle or terrible illness in which we are sick in the middle of the day. However, the monks thought of such noonday destruction in terms of what they called "sloth," that is, not laziness so much as a deep despair in which we can no longer enjoy what is good or rejoice in the beauty of the day. When even the blue sky and the bright sunlight depress us, then we really are captive to "the

10. The phrase is Neil Postman's. See his *Amusing Ourselves to Death: Public Discourse in the Age of Show Business* (London: Penguin Books), 1986.

destruction that wastes at noonday." It is contempt for life's goodness, contempt not for what is cheap or trivial but contempt for what is good and true and beautiful. It is one thing to say, "I do not want read the *Iliad*," but it is another thing to say "the *Iliad* is not worth reading." When we reject God's good gifts, then we always risk that terrible boredom known as "the destruction that wastes at noonday." Sometimes when I read about a young person committing suicide or dying of a drug overdose, I wonder whether he or she was a victim of "the destruction that wastes at noonday." It is an ever-present threat, especially in a culture that works so frantically to keep from being bored. The psalmist thinks, however, that one of God's greatest gifts is simple joy in life, the contentment and surprise that come from discovering the beauty in small things, the endless mystery underneath every rock.

The other day I read a story of a woman in Houston who was a member of a large Presbyterian congregation there. She had a successful business and was doing well, but she was unhappy. One day she left her business and went to her pastor and asked to be put to work. As I write this, she is teaching English as a second language and helping to administer a tutoring program that the Presbyterian Church conducts in Piedras Negras, Mexico. In an interview, she said that she had never felt so free, so happy in her life. She had been set free from "the destruction that wastes at noonday" by the gift of service to Jesus Christ. That is freedom indeed.

The psalm ends with God's promise to protect us wherever we go and whenever we get into trouble. "Those who love me, I will deliver; I will protect those who know my name." An old hymn sings, "Trust and obey, for there's no other way." There really is not. And the God who shelters us under his wings will care for us, protecting us even from ourselves and our own follies, setting us free for life in him.

Let us pray: Help me to trust in you, O Lord, and help me find that freedom that makes life interesting, purposeful, and generous. Be with me today in all that I do. Walk with me in the midst of my troubles and fears. And give me your peace. I pray this in Jesus Christ's name. Amen.

NOTES

Psalm 100

Make a joyful noise to the Lord, all the earth.
  Worship the Lord with gladness, come into his
  presence with singing.

Know that the Lord is God!
  It is he that made us, and we are his;
  We are his people, and the sheep of his pasture.

Enter his gates with thanksgiving, and his courts
  with praise.
  Give thanks to him, bless his name.

For the Lord is good; his steadfast love endures forever,
  And his faithfulness to all generations.

DAY 20

PSALM 100

THERE WAS A TIME WHEN THE BOOK OF PSALMS WAS PRETTY MUCH THE HYMNBOOK FOR THE REFORMED FAITH. WE SANG ONLY PSALMS OR PSALMS PUT INTO English rhymes and meter. "Old Hundredth" was the metrical version of this psalm, and we still sing it in worship today:

> All people that on earth do dwell, Sing to the Lord
>   with cheerful voice;
> Him serve with mirth, His praise forth tell, Come ye
>   before him and rejoice.
>
> Know that the Lord is God indeed; Without our aid
>   He did us make;
> We are his folk, He doth us feed, And for his sheep he
>   doth us take.
>
> O enter then His gates with praise, Approach with
>   joy his courts unto;
> Praise, laud and bless his name always, For it is
>   seemly so to do.
>
> For why? The Lord our God is good, His mercy is
>   forever sure;

*His truth at all times firmly stood, And shall from
age to age endure.*[11]

A wonderful hymn and a wonderful psalm. It is a psalm
that invites everyone to "make a joyful noise," to voice the
praise and thanksgiving we have within us as children of our
heavenly Father, as creatures of the one who has made us.
"Serve the Lord with gladness! Come into his presence with
singing!" Have you ever wondered why people who worship God sing? Why is God not satisfied with just our prose,
an essay, perhaps, or even a conversation? Why does he
invite us to sing? I suspect it has something to do with our
hearts. Nothing moves us quite like music, and nothing gets
hold of us quite like a song. This morning, coming to work,
I heard a love song on the radio that was popular when I was
in high school. Believe me, it took me back. And as I was
driving, I found myself singing along with its lyrics, and for
a moment, I was back in high school, wondering why the
girl I wanted to ask to the prom did not seem to know I
existed. Music does that to you. When we sing our praises
to God, we are singing a love song. As with all such songs,
the music compels not just our thoughts or minds or even
our time, but compels our hearts. We give ourselves to God
in music. This is why we come into his presence with
singing.

What do we sing? The psalmist reminds us that the Lord
is God. "It is he that made us, and we are his." It is important for us to sing this tune because we often sing other
songs, songs that suggest that we are self-made, that we
belong to ourselves and can continually reinvent ourselves.
Our culture specializes in singing "a song of myself." But
such songs, in the end, are never joyful. They finally end up

11. *The Presbyterian Hymnal*, #220; William Kethe.

as solos or, worse, as just a constant noise. I once heard a person say that in hell there is no music, only noise. For music to work, there must be harmony, a singing together and a blending of different voices. Such a harmony reminds us that we do not make ourselves. Our lives are songs that God has written, and we spend our days trying to learn to sing that song. And we find that, sooner or later, God's song sounds best when it is harmonized with all the other songs God has written in the lives of those around us. "We are his people and the sheep of his pasture."

The psalmist concludes this great song of thanksgiving with the words that "the Lord is good." God is good. Sometimes we have to be reminded of that because we forget that God is good. In C. S. Lewis's children's book, *The Lion, the Witch and the Wardrobe,* Susan, one of the children, asks Mr. Beaver whether the Lion, Aslan, is entirely safe. Aslan, the Lion, is very much a figure of Christ in the book. Mr. Beaver replies, "Safe? . . . Who said anything about safe? 'Course he isn't safe. But he's good."[12] That is a good way to think about God. God is not entirely safe. He may involve you in a heap of trouble and get you into situations in which you could never imagine yourself. To follow one who was himself crucified has always been a dangerous business, and we do not do ourselves any favors by pretending that the Christian life is merely safe. But it is good, just as God is good. And God's goodness "endures forever." His goodness redeems the messes we live in and make. His goodness heals our wounds and mends our broken hearts. "For the Lord is good; his steadfast love endures forever, and his faithfulness to all generations."

That is why we sing.

12. C. S. Lewis, "The Lion, the Witch and the Wardrobe," in *The Essential C. S. Lewis*, ed. Lyle Dorsett (New York: Touchstone, 1996), 93.

Let us pray: Give me a song in my heart this day, O Lord, that I may sing your praises and declare myself your own. Be with me all day, and even at the end of the day, help me sing your faithfulness and remember your love. I pray this in the name of Jesus Christ, who is your faithfulness and has become my song. Amen.

NOTES

Psalm 103

*Bless the Lord, O my soul, and all that is within me,
    bless his holy name.*
*Bless the Lord, O my soul, and do not forget all his
    benefits—*
    Who forgives all your iniquity,
    Who heals all your diseases,
    Who redeems your life from the Pit,
    Who crowns you with steadfast love and mercy,
    Who satisfies you with good as long as you live
    So that your youth is renewed like the eagle's.

*The Lord works vindication and justice for all who
    are oppressed.*
*He made known his ways to Moses, his acts to the
    people of Israel.*
The Lord is merciful and gracious,
    Slow to anger and abounding in steadfast love.
*He will not always accuse, nor will he keep his anger
    forever.*
He does not deal with us according to our sins,
    Nor repay us according to our iniquities.
For as the heavens are high above the earth,
    *So great is his steadfast love toward those who
    fear him;*
As far as the east is from the west,
    So far he removes our transgressions from us.
As a father has compassion for his children,
    *So the Lord has compassion for those who fear
    him.*

For he knows how we were made; he remembers that
we are dust.

As for mortals, their days are like grass;
They flourish like a flower of the field;
For the wind passes over it, and it is gone, and its
place knows it no more.
But the steadfast love of the Lord is from everlasting
to everlasting
On those who fear him,
And his righteousness to children's children, to
those who keep his covenant
And remember to do his commandments.

The Lord has established his throne in the heavens,
And his kingdom rules over all.
Bless the Lord, O you his angels,
You mighty ones who do his bidding, obedient to
his spoken word.
Bless the Lord, all his hosts, his ministers that do his
will.
Bless the Lord, all his works, in all places of his
dominion.
Bless the Lord, O my soul.

DAY 21

PSALM 103

THIS WAS MY MOTHER'S FAVORITE PSALM. IT BEGINS WITH THE WORDS, "BLESS THE LORD, O MY SOUL; AND ALL THAT IS WITHIN ME, BLESS HIS HOLY NAME." IT BEGINS BY blessing the Lord and not by blessing "all that is within me." The Lord comes first, and it is in blessing his holy name that "all that is within me" finds its rightful place in worship and life. Often today, we hear a blessing of all that is within me, and only then, if then, do we hear any blessing of the Lord. But the psalmist wants to say what is most important first and wants us to know that the Lord is the source of all blessing. In blessing his holy name, we can find our true place, our true selves. That is why we worship: to orient ourselves to reality. Worship directs us to true north. Without worship, we lose our bearings and come to think that our lives begin with the "blessing of all that is within me," something our culture has no trouble believing. This psalm, like all scripture, is countercultural that way. It begins by blessing the Lord.

Then it invites us to remember how this Lord has in fact blessed us: "Who forgives all your iniquity, who heals all your diseases, who redeems your life from the Pit, who crowns you with steadfast love and mercy, who satisfies you with good as long as you live so that your youth is renewed like the eagle's."

Quite a list. The Lord forgives: That is the first blessing the psalmist mentions, and without it there are no others. We cannot live a day without such forgiveness. His forgiveness is grace on grace, a grace that gives us courage to try again even when we have failed miserably, a grace that enables us to get up in the morning and start a new day.

The Lord heals. He heals our bodies and our souls; he repairs the fabric of our lives. He gives strength for life. How could we live without his healing?

The Lord "redeems your life from the Pit." The psalmist knows that there are times in our lives when we hit rock bottom, when we suffer from black depression or are in a tight spot from which there appears to be no escape. Time and again, the psalms sing of the deliverance of the Lord. He snatches us out of the pit; he makes dry land appear; he sets us free.

He "crowns you with steadfast love and mercy." We should think of this more than we do, for it sometimes comes as a surprise to us that the Lord is proud of us, that he loves us, that he "crowns" us with his favor. We specialize at times in thinking ourselves poor, miserable sinners. But God does not. He sees us shining in the light of Jesus Christ, so that even our struggles become luminescent. When we confess our faith in him, he is proud of us. He crowns us as kings, as a "royal priesthood," "God's own people." (1 Pet. 2:9). Martin Luther once said that when a person has prayed the Lord's Prayer and confessed his or her faith in Jesus Christ, he or she should not go home with a long face looking down at the ground, but with head held high. Such a person has spoken the truth and lives in the truth. Such a person is a person after God's own heart. God is not ashamed to be our God.

This psalm goes on to note that "the Lord is merciful and gracious, slow to anger and abounding in steadfast love."

The good news is that "He does not deal with us according to our sins, nor repay us according to our iniquities. For as the heavens are high above the earth, so great is his steadfast love toward those who fear him; as far as the east is from the west, so far he removes our transgressions from us." This is the heart of the gospel, our assurance of pardon. The God who does all of this is not just any god, but the one who "made known his ways to Moses, his acts to the people of Israel." He is the God of Scripture's story, the God of Israel and the church, the God whom we cannot know unless we are engrafted into this story and joined to Christ's body.

The psalmist concludes by reminding us that many things change, but not the steadfast love of the Lord. It is "from everlasting to everlasting." *Steadfast* is a word the Bible uses a lot, but it is not a word we use very much. It means, simply, that God always shows up. Always. Even when we do not. Even when we are not in a very good mood. Even when we are sick or tired or weary of ourselves. God shows up and loves us. He is steadfast, rock solid. You can count on him. Which is why the psalm ends with the words with which it began: "Bless the Lord, O my soul."

Let us pray: Thank you, Lord, for being there for me, for loving me and forgiving me, for healing me and watching over me, for making my life something more than just grass withering in the field. Thank you for engrafting me into your church. I would bless you. I would bless you every day and sing to you songs of praise. Give me such a song this day, I pray, and give me the strength to sing to you with my life. Amen.

NOTES

Psalm 119 : 1–30; 105

*Happy are those whose way is blameless, who walk in
the law of the Lord.*
*Happy are those who keep his decrees, who seek him
with their whole heart,*
  Who also do no wrong, but walk in his ways.
You have commanded your precepts to be kept diligently.
*O that my ways may be steadfast in keeping your
statutes!*
Then I shall not be put to shame,
  Having my eyes fixed on all your commandments.
*I will praise you with an upright heart, when I learn
your righteous ordinances.*
I will observe your statutes; do not utterly forsake me.

How can young people keep their way pure?
By guarding it according to your word.
*With my whole heart I seek you; do not let me stray
from your commandments.*
*I treasure your word in my heart, so that I may not
sin against you.*
Blessed are you, O Lord; teach me your statutes.
With my lips I declare all the ordinances of your mouth.
*I delight in the way of your decrees as much as in all
riches.*
*I will meditate on your precepts, and fix my eyes on
your ways.*
I will delight in your statutes;
I will not forget your word.

*Deal bountifully with your servant, so that I may live
and observe your word.*

Open my eyes, so that I may behold wondrous things
    out of your law.
I live as an alien in the land; do not hide your
    commandments from me.
My soul is consumed with longing for your
    ordinances at all times.
You rebuke the insolent, accursed ones, who wander
    from your commandments;
    Take away from me their scorn and contempt, for
    I have kept your decrees.
Even though princes sit plotting against me,
    Your servant will meditate on your statutes.
Your decrees are my delight, they are my counselors.

My soul clings to the dust; revive me according to
    your word.
When I told of my ways, you answered me; teach me
    your statutes.
Make me understand the way of your precepts,
    And I will meditate on your wondrous works.
My soul melts away for sorrow; strengthen me
    according to your word.
Put false ways far from me; and graciously teach me
    your law.
I have chosen the way of faithfulness; I set your
    ordinances before me.

Your word is a lamp to my feet and a light to my path.

DAY 22

—◦—

PSALM 119

THIS IS THE LONGEST PSALM IN THE BIBLE, AND SOME
WOULD SAY THE MOST BORING. IT APPEARS TO BE WRIT-
TEN BY A LEGALIST RATHER ON THE ORDER OF ERNIE'S
friend, Bert, who is as rapturous about the law as Bert is
about his paper clips. The rest of us have a hard time appre-
ciating their beauty.

In Hebrew, the psalm resembles something of an acrostic
puzzle. It is divided into twenty-two stanzas of eight lines
each, with each stanza beginning with the corresponding letter of the Hebrew alphabet. The first stanza, for example,
begins with the letter *aleph,* and the next with *beth,* and so on
down to *tau,* the last letter. There are only twenty-two letters
in the Hebrew alphabet, the vowels being missing, or rather,
indicated by what are called "points" (i. e., minute dots or
signs in a word indicating how it is to be pronounced). This
psalm is a song of praise to God. God is mentioned or referred
to in every one of the 176 verses. Particularly, this psalm gives
thanks for God's law, a word that appears frequently, along
with several other variants (e. g., "testimonies," "ordinances,"
"ways," "precepts," "commandments," "statutes").

In English, however, the psalm can sound dull, even
monotonous. When read all the way through at one sitting,
it resembles one of those songs we might sing on a long trip
to pass the time away ("99 bottles of beer on the wall, 99
bottles of beer, take one down pass it around, 98 bottles of

beer on the wall"). Such a song is hardly sung for its intrinsic beauty but more as a challenge to see if we can get through it.

However, the psalmist was not just playing games. He was passionately in love with God's law. The word, "law," *torah,* can also mean a word that hits its target, a word of truth. The psalmist believed that God's word was truth, the truth about this world, the truth about himself, the truth. This truth was profoundly good news—not bad, not pharisaical, not conditional, not mixed, but good, happy news. So this psalmist went a bit crazy, as people who are in love sometimes do. He wrote a love letter to the God whose truth was so wonderful that it embodied itself in everyday things, in an everyday way, in everyday laws. This song celebrates truth incarnate in our world, the kind of truth incarnate in Jesus Christ, the Word made flesh.

My favorite line in the psalm is the most often quoted line, Verse 105: "Thy word is a lamp to my feet and a light to my path." God's word helps us see. Without that word, we are like people driving down the highway without their lights on, careening down the road endangering themselves and others. God's word helps us see and protects us and our neighbors. His word enables a community to exist, to live. His word is a gift, "a lamp to my feet."

Such a simple sentiment may seem buried in this overflowing of praise, but it is really the most wonderful prayer of thanksgiving, a prayer that acknowledges the other major theme of this psalm, namely, that God is steadfast and sure. His is a light that never goes out, "a lamp unto my feet, a light to my path." If the psalm contained nothing more than this thought, it would be worth praying. If it can help us grasp some of the passion God regularly inspires in his people, then it would be worth praying again and again.

Let us pray: Heavenly Father, thank you for your gift of truth. My own life seems so full of uncertainties and at times even falsehoods. And I hear lies every day telling me I am valuable only if I have money to spend or appear with the right people or dress in the right clothes. Your word is truth, inside and out. Thank you for that word, a word that exposes every lie and sheds light on my path. Give me the grace to follow your word, to fall head over heels in love with your word. For your word is "a lamp to my feet and a light to my path." Amen.

NOTES

Psalm 16

Protect me, O God, for in you I take refuge.
I say to the Lord, "You are my Lord; I have no good
    apart from you."

As for the holy ones in the land, they are the
    noble, in whom is all my delight.

Those who choose another god multiply their sorrows;
    Their drink offerings of blood I will not pour out
    Or take their names upon my lips.

The Lord is my chosen portion and my cup; you hold
    my lot.
The boundary lines have fallen for me in pleasant
    places;
I have a goodly heritage.

I bless the Lord who gives me counsel;
    In the night also my heart instructs me.
I keep the Lord always before me;
    Because he is at my right hand, I shall not be
    moved.

Therefore my heart is glad, and my soul rejoices;
    My body also rests secure.
For you do not give me up to Sheol,
    Or let your faithful one see the Pit.

You show me the path of life.
In your presence there is fullness of joy;
In your right hand are pleasures forevermore.

DAY 23

— ◆ ◆ —

PSALM 16

S OME YEARS AGO, WHEN MY UNCLE DIED, I ATTENDED HIS
MEMORIAL SERVICE, WHICH WAS HELD IN A SMALL PRESBY-
TERIAN CHURCH. HE HAD PASTORED FOR FORTY YEARS OR
so, and he died while pastoring this church in South Texas.
At his memorial service, this psalm was read. It was the first
time I had ever "heard" it. Of course, I had heard it before,
but either I was not paying attention or my dullness proved
impenetrable on those occasions. This time I really heard
the psalm, and it seemed fitting to me that it was read at the
memorial service of one who took so much pleasure in
being alive.

The psalm begins with the confession that "I have no good
apart from you." Anything I have ever achieved, any triumph
I may ever have enjoyed, if it is not rooted in or tending
toward God's liberating gift of life in Jesus Christ, then it is
just a clanging cymbal that announces a deeper imprison-
ment to self. All the goods I have—people who love me,
health and strength in body and mind, a heart made to love
God—all these goods come from God and are gifts beyond
the imagining. "I have no good apart from you."

However, the psalmist knows that not everyone thinks as
he does. There are those who choose other gods, those who
worship themselves and make their own appetites the con-
trolling factor in their lives. They live from infidelity to

infidelity, from betrayal to betrayal, but the result is not happiness. Rather, they "multiply their sorrows."

Simone Weil, a Jewish woman who came to a deep understanding of the Christian faith, once wrote: "Imaginary evil is romantic and varied, full of charm; imaginary good is tiresome and flat. Real evil, however, is dreary, monotonous, barren. Real good is always new, marvelous, intoxicating."[13] We often imagine human sinfulness as glamorous, slightly dangerous, perhaps even fun. The prospect of no constraints, no obligations, no entangling relationships seems alluring to us. But the psalmist is more realistic than we are. What we call "freedom" is in reality, he thinks, pretty grim. There is little glamour in drug addiction, or in an alcoholic haze, or in the abuse of a child. Faithfulness to God, which we often imagine to be tedious if not boring, resembles, he thinks, true happiness. In such a life, we find joy in being bound to another whose life entangles us in a life of generosity and self-giving. A mother whose life is entangled in the lives of her children is happy; a husband and wife whose lives together are entangled with each other in a marriage of deep commitment are truly free; a student who falls in love with learning and whose life is ever after entangled in the enterprise (and hard work) of exploring the life of the mind possesses a wonderful gift. All such folk are far happier than one who knows no entanglement with others but must deal with the boredom of self. Hell is a lonely place. Heaven, in contrast, is always convivial, full of interesting people and lots and lots of laughter.

"The Lord is my chosen portion and my cup; you hold my lot. The boundary lines have fallen for me in pleasant places; I have a goodly heritage."

13. As cited in "A Martyr Is Born," by J. Bottum, in *The Weekly Standard*, 10 May, 1999; 13.

The "boundary lines" of your life have fallen in pleasant places. You are loved. This church has nurtured you and taught you. Your family has surrounded you with love. When you have fallen down or hurt yourself, there has always been someone, a mom or a dad, a coach or friend, to help you get back up. One of the great gifts of the faith is to receive the heritage of Israel's story, and with it the church, the people who know what it is like to fall and be picked up by others, to receive grace and to live in the love of a family, a community of faith. This heritage is not everyone's by nature, but it belongs to everyone through the grace of baptism. A part of that heritage is this book of Psalms. It belongs to you too; it is a gift. It will pick you up and shape your life in a Christ-like way through its singing and confessing and hoping. "The boundary lines have fallen for me in pleasant places."

"Therefore my heart is glad." Therefore, we can sing. Therefore, we can risk imitating the birds of the air and the lilies of the field and simply live and bloom and fly as God's good and happy creatures. God is the source of true happiness. We think sometimes that God is the source only of doing right, or of moral seriousness, or of great sacrifice, or even of painful punishment and judgment. But the psalmist sings of the God who makes our hearts sing. That is what is so hard for us to believe at times. "You show me the path of life. In your presence there is fullness of joy; in your right hand are pleasures forevermore."

In his book, *The Screwtape Letters*, C. S. Lewis reminded us that God invented the good things, not the devil. Satan can only spoil the good things God has made; he cannot make a single pleasure. Pleasure is God's invention, and when we are truly enjoying ourselves, then we are on God's turf, not the devil's. To be sure, we can twist such pleasures so that they become ends in themselves, but then they are twisted and become means that serve our purposes. As pleasures, though, as simple gifts, they are always God's, and they come from his hand.[14] "In your right hand are pleasures forevermore." What a great embarrassment for Calvinists like your pastor to be told that it is all right to smile. After all, Jesus *is* the victor!

Let us pray: Help me to enjoy this day: the sunshine and the rain, the trees and the sky, the good things to eat, the gift of rest and sleep, the joy of working and studying, the blessings of play. Help me to enjoy the gift of being alive, for such a gift comes from your own hands. I offer this prayer in the name of Jesus Christ the Lord. Amen.

14. C. S. Lewis, *The Screwtape Letters* (New York: Macmillan, 1944), 49.

Psalm 24

The earth is the Lord's and all that is in it,
The world, and those who live in it;
For he has founded it on the seas, and established it
on the rivers.

Who shall ascend the hill of the Lord? And who shall
stand in his holy place?
Those who have clean hands and pure hearts,
Who do not lift up their souls to what is false,
And do not swear deceitfully.
They will receive blessing from the Lord,
And vindication from the God of their salvation.
Such is the company of those who seek him,
Who seek the face of the God of Jacob.

Lift up your heads, O gates! And be lifted up, O
ancient doors!
That the King of glory may come in.
Who is the King of glory?
The Lord, strong and mighty, the Lord, mighty in
battle.
Lift up your heads, O gates! And be lifted up, O
ancient doors!
That the King of glory may come in.
Who is this King of glory?
The Lord of hosts, he is the King of glory.

DAY 24

〜

PSALM 24

THIS PSALM IS ABOUT WORSHIP. SO MANY OF THE PSALMS SEEM TO TAKE DELIGHT IN SIMPLY PRAISING GOD, IN WORSHIPING. THIS PSALM BEGINS BY PRAISING GOD FOR the earth, for all creation. "The earth is the Lord's and all that is in it, the world, and those who live in it." Israel's faith in God was no private matter. God was not a personal good-luck charm or even a mere national deity, but God was Lord of all. To be sure, God had called Israel alone to be his people, but just so, God's intent was that Israel be a "light to the nations," so that all the nations of the earth would be blessed by Israel's life and come to acknowledge God as Lord. So the Old Testament begins, not with Exodus, that is, not with God's deliverance of Israel, but with Genesis, that is, with God's creation of the whole world. Israel's God is Lord of all.

Who shall worship such a gracious and loving God? Who has a right to enter into God's presence? We do not often think of worship that way. More often, we think of worship as a duty or chore. This psalm is different. It asks which of us has a right to be in the presence of God. The answer it gives is not terribly comforting: "Those who have clean hands and a pure heart, who do not lift up their souls to what is false, and do not swear deceitfully." Oh. If the only folks who can enter into God's presence are those who have "clean hands and a pure heart," then I really have no business being in worship.

If worship is this difficult, then who can worship? Are we not all people of unclean lips and hearts? Yet the psalmist seems to think that worship is nevertheless possible. Indeed, that is why he sings, because he thinks God has made worship possible. The holy God has made an unholy people holy, just as he has made an unclean people pure. God makes our broken lives whole. The person who goes to worship, then, "will receive blessing from the Lord, and vindication from the God of their salvation."

In Flannery O'Connor's short story "Revelation," a character named Ruby Turpin thinks she is clean but discovers by God's grace and an angry college student that she is not. In fact, she has been blind to her own selfishness and silliness for some time, and her discovery that God is about something more than her self-esteem is shattering. Late in the story, however, she receives a revelation and envisions all the folk she had so easily dismissed as "beyond the pale" entering heaven before her. But she sees herself and her husband Claud following them, "marching behind the others with great dignity, accountable as they had always been for good order and common sense and respectable behavior. They alone were [singing] on key. Yet she could see by their shocked and altered faces that even their virtues were being burned away."[15] A better description of the blessing that we receive from the Lord can scarcely be imagined. Worship brings us into the presence of the one who not only overcomes our tarnished lives with his forgiveness, but also saves us from terrible captivity to our virtues. Ruby's problem was, like the Pharisees, that she thought her virtues were what made her attractive to God. She could "do"

15. Flannery O'Connor, "Revelation," in *Flannery O'Connor: The Complete Stories* (New York: Farrar, Straus, and Giroux, 1987), 508.

virtue, and so, she thought, she would not need any miracle of grace to redeem her. Her shattering discovery was that the only way we come into God's presence is through grace, a grace that relentlessly exposes our sinful efforts to use even our virtues to avoid God's mysterious love. Such a grace always burns our virtues away.

In truth, there is only one who has "clean hands and a pure heart," only one who can give us his holiness in exchange for our selfishness. He is the one who is worthy to open the scroll and undo the seals. He is the one who can open the gates and lift up the ancient doors so that true worship is really possible and sinners can find a place at his table. This psalm is subtitled "a psalm of David," and it is. It is particularly a psalm of David's son, Jesus. In Handel's *Messiah,* one of the great choruses is based on just this psalm: "Who is the King of glory?" The answer comes resoundingly back, "The Lord of hosts, He is the King of glory!"

In John's gospel, Jesus tells his disciples, "I am the door." Just so does he open himself to us, becoming for us the door we enter to worship and to life. It is a gift to ascend the hill of the Lord and follow him into worship.

Let us pray: Day by day, Lord, give me strength to follow Jesus Christ. So may I find in him my joy, my hope, my life. This I pray in his name. Amen.

Psalm 124

If it had not been the Lord who was on our side
   —let Israel now say—
If it had not been the Lord who was on our side,
   When our enemies attacked us,
Then they would have swallowed us up alive,
   When their anger was kindled against us;
Then the flood would have swept us away,
   The torrent would have gone over us;
Then over us would have gone the raging waters.

Blessed be the Lord, who has not given us as prey to
   their teeth.
We have escaped like a bird from the snare of the
   fowlers;
   The snare is broken, and we have escaped.

Our help is in the name of the Lord, who made
   heaven and earth.

DAY 25

PSALM 124

MANY OF THE PSALMS ARE SUNG BY PEOPLE WHO ARE IN TROUBLE. BIG TROUBLE. SOMETIMES THEY WANT GOD TO WAKE UP AND TAKE NOTICE OF THEIR TROUBLE AND DO something about it. Sometimes they ask how long they must suffer, how long they must endure. But sometimes they sing because they have been delivered, got out of a tight spot by the Lord who has suddenly appeared as their defender, indeed, as their savior. At such moments, they sing as the author of this psalm sings: "We have escaped like a bird from the snare of the fowlers; the snare is broken, and we have escaped."

Some time ago, a lady in the church I was pastoring had cancer. She had fought it gamely and with chemotherapy and great courage on her part; she apparently beat it. Time passed, and she resumed her life. After a while, however, she began to have a painful swelling in her abdomen. Because of her history, the doctors did extensive tests looking for a recurrence of the cancer. They were sure this was another tumor. The results, however, were inconclusive. Exploratory surgery was scheduled, and I drove to Houston to be with her and her husband. I had talked with him on the phone the night before, and he was worried. He too felt certain that it was a recurrence of the cancer. I drove to Houston that morning feeling low myself, hoping against hope. But as I walked into the waiting room, the husband greeted me with a big smile. The doctors had found an abscess on her appendix, he told me. It had been growing for some time and could easily be removed. There was no cancer. He started dancing around the waiting room, laughing and singing, like a bird that had escaped the snare of the fowler.

"The snare is broken, and we have escaped." There are times in life when we say we dodged a bullet, times when we sense that by rights our number should have been up. We should have been hit when we inadvertently ran that red light, but we were not. We should have been penalized for not doing our homework that day, but we were not. We should have been docked for coming to work late, but we were not. Sometimes we think we were just lucky. But if we think about it for very long, we might conclude that maybe there really is something to this grace business. Maybe grace is all around us, and we are saved by grace every day: saved from accidents, from diseases, from the worst things we could do to ourselves. Could that be why Israel insisted that God was gracious? He overlooks our failures. Were he not on our side, to quote the psalmist, "If it had not been the Lord who was on our side, when our enemies attacked us, then they would have swallowed us up alive."

Israel saw her whole life as a matter of grace, of being unaccountably delivered. It was not because she was more numerous than others, or smarter or more powerful, but because God loved her. When she looked back on her life, she could only confess that God was in the middle of it, hidden at times but always bringing about her good. Other nations have had great armies and large empires and powerful weapons. Israel for the past 2,500 years has, until recently, had none of these things. But whereas Rome fell, whereas nearly all ancient peoples were absorbed by other cultures, Israel in the life of the Jewish people still lives. When Frederick the Great asked Voltaire for a proof of

God, he is supposed to have replied, "Sire, the Jews." What he meant by that was that there was no way for this little people ever to have survived, much less to have flourished, were it not for God's intervening hand.

Sometimes you just have to sing in gratitude for God's goodness. In one of Philip Yancey's essays, he argued that if atheists demand that Christians explain the origin of suffering, then ought not atheists have to account for the origin of pleasure in the world? Why are there beautiful sunsets? Why does food taste good? Why does love make you giddy? Could a world not have been constructed just as efficiently and purposefully without such joys? The answer, of course, is in Yancey's words, that "a good and loving God would naturally want his creatures to experience delight, joy, and personal fulfillment."[16] Sometimes, after you escape like a bird from the snare of the fowler, you just have to sing, you just have to thank God for the goodness of his marvelous and surprising gifts.

The psalm ends with the words with which we begin every worship service. "Our help is in the name of the Lord, who made heaven and earth." That is how the people of God should begin worship, always confessing at the outset that we cannot even worship aright without the help of God's astonishing deliverance. We are saved by grace, like birds who have escaped from those who would trap them in a culture of self. How wonderful to be able to fly, to be able to worship, to be able to dance! "Can you believe it?" my friend asked me that day in the hospital waiting room. "My wife is going to live; she is going to be well!" "Our help is in the name of the Lord, who made heaven and earth."

Let us pray: Our Father, for your gracious love, receive my thanks. Help me to take joy in this day, to be as happy as Snoopy is when he dances. So may I dance this day, forgetting

16. Philip Yancey, *I Was Just Wondering* (Grand Rapids: Eerdmans, 1989), 32.

self and rejoicing in you. And then, when this day comes to an end and I am tired and sleepy, give me rest in your grace and sleep in your loving arms. In the name of Jesus Christ, I pray. Amen.

NOTES

Psalm 69: 1–3; 6–12; 16–22; 28–33

Save me, O God, for the waters have come up to my neck.
I sink in deep mire, where there is no foothold;
I have come into deep waters, and the flood sweeps
     over me.
I am weary with my crying; my throat is parched.
My eyes grow dim with waiting for my God.

Do not let those who hope in you be put to shame
     because of me,
          O Lord God of hosts;
Do not let those who seek you be dishonored because
     of me,
          O God of Israel.
It is for your sake that I have borne reproach, that
     shame has covered my face.
I have become a stranger to my kindred, an alien to
     my mother's children.

It is zeal for your house that has consumed me;
The insults of those who insult you have fallen on me.
When I humbled my soul with fasting, they insulted
     me for doing so.
When I made sackcloth my clothing, I became a
     byword to them.
I am the subject of gossip for those who sit in the gate,
     And the drunkards make songs about me.

Answer me, O Lord, for your steadfast love is good;
     According to your abundant mercy, turn to me.
Do not hide your face from your servant,

For I am in distress—make haste to answer me.
Draw near to me, redeem me, set me free because of
  my enemies.

You know the insults I receive, and my shame and
  dishonor;
    My foes are all known to you.
Insults have broken my heart, so that I am in
  despair.
I looked for pity, but there was none; and for
  comforters, but I found none.
They gave me poison for food,
    And for my thirst they gave me vinegar to drink.

Let their table be a trap for them, a snare for their
  allies.

Let them be blotted out of the book of the living;
    Let them not be enrolled among the righteous.
But I am lowly and in pain; let your salvation, O
  God, protect me.

I will praise the name of God with a song; I will
  magnify him with thanksgiving.
This will please the Lord more than an ox or a bull
  with horns and hoofs.
Let the oppressed see it and be glad; you who seek
  God, let your hearts revive.
For the Lord hears the needy, and does not despise
  his own that are in bonds.

_____

147

DAY 26

—◦—

PSALM 69

HERE IS ANOTHER PSALM BY A PERSON UP TO HER NECK IN TROUBLE: "SAVE ME, O GOD! FOR THE WATERS HAVE COME UP TO MY NECK."

But her trouble is not cancer, or some prospect of loss. No, her trouble is her loneliness. She is lonely in a culture that celebrates unfaithfulness, lonely because she has been faithful. What has her faithfulness got her? Loneliness and hurt. "I am weary with my crying; my throat is parched. My eyes grow dim with waiting for my God." When I am faithful and true, and others are not, indeed, when others flaunt their self-centeredness and seem to flourish, where is God?

As I write this, there are those who are asking, "Where is the outrage?" The leader of our nation has admitted to an inappropriate relationship with a young intern in the Oval Office and has lied, and there are seemingly no consequences. Indeed, if anything, the president seems to flourish; his popularity remains higher than ever. Perhaps he is not the problem. Perhaps there is something wrong with us. Perhaps this is merely a trivial matter. After all, everything, we are often told, is political, and there can be no doubt that many enjoy remarking on the failings of the powerful. Why risk being outraged by such behavior? Are we so pure?

"It is for your sake that I have borne reproach, that shame has covered my face. I have become a stranger to my kindred, an alien to my mother's children."

It is a measure of how domesticated our faith has become that we are sometimes surprised, even offended, by the notion of faith incurring enmity. One of the songs I learned as a child was entitled "Friends, Friends, Friends!" a song about friendship's reciprocity. "I love my friends and they love me, I help my friends and they help me," we sang cheerfully in Sunday School. It seemed a pretty good deal. But sometimes the faith that is rooted in the story of the cross has to reckon with the fact that faith makes enemies rather than friends. Indeed, faith can be a dangerous business. A colleague of mine here at the church, George Kluber, once parodied the pop psychology of our day by envisioning Jesus on the cross saying: "Hey, if I'm okay and you're okay, what am I doing up here on the cross?" Exactly. The unpleasant truth is that some people *hated* Jesus. They wanted him dead.

On a pleasant Sunday morning in worship, such visceral hatred seems out of place, an unpleasantness that we seek to disguise with lovely flowers and beautiful music. But it is at least worth asking the question why people were so angry with Jesus that they put him to death. For it is in Jesus' name that we are gathered in worship and find ourselves, potentially at least, exposed to the same risk he was.

"It is zeal for your house that has consumed me." This verse, Psalm 69:9, is remembered by Jesus' disciples, according to John's Gospel (John 2:17) on the occasion of Jesus' cleansing of the temple. "He told those who were selling the doves, 'Take these things out of here! Stop making my Father's house a marketplace!'" (John 2:16) Jesus' embodiment of a faithful and true life before God set him at odds with a world eager to use faith for its own purposes. You cleanse a few temples, and people get mad at you. It eventually got Jesus the cross. And there, the creed reminds us, "he suffered." There he was surrounded by his enemies who gloated and taunted him. All of sudden, Psalm 69 sounds like the Passion narrative of Jesus' last days: "Let me be delivered from my enemies and from the deep waters. Do not let the flood sweep over me, or the deep swallow me up, or the Pit close its mouth over me." (Ps. 69:14, 15) If you read the rest of this psalm, you will see why the gospel writers who had to describe Jesus' crucifixion thought of this psalm so readily. "Insults have broken my heart, so that I am in despair. I looked for pity, but there was none; and for comforters, but I found none. They gave me poison for food, and for my thirst they gave me vinegar to drink." The gospel writers who cited this passage in their own accounts of Jesus' death did not think that Jesus was just a lonely man trying to do good. They thought of Jesus in terms of Israel's life, so that Jesus embodied what Israel was called to be. In fulfilling that role, Jesus became an offering for the whole world. This psalm is not just about Jesus, but he is in some sense its subject. He is the one praying this psalm. He is its author.

When you read a psalm like this or try to pray with it, you must keep in mind that Jesus is the one who is speaking. The psalm, I know, is called "a psalm of David" and was written long before Jesus was born in Bethlehem. But the early church thought that its words were in fact the words of Jesus and by the power of the Holy Spirit were words best understood in terms of Christ's praying of them. For us to pray these words, then, is for us to enter into his life, to be drawn into his offering of himself on behalf of the world, and so begin to see our lives as offerings, too. In that way, we begin to share in Christ's ministry and to read our own sufferings in the light of his. Such sharing is a gift. It is, indeed, the opposite of loneliness or cultivating a sense of martyrdom. Rather, such sharing becomes a way of praying, even of becoming a prayer in which in Christ we offer ourselves to God the Father.

The psalm ends with a word of thanksgiving, even a word of confidence that God "hears the needy, and does not despise his own that are in bonds."

This is good news for all who suffer "for righteousness' sake." God does not leave us to our own devices or abandon us to what the world calls "justice." Instead he sets us free. Instead he gives us life in Christ. Not even Jesus died alone, but even at death he was in the company of sinners, a fellowship of the redeemed. The way of faithfulness is indeed lonely at times. No one can deny that. But this way is not finally one of isolated and heroic loneliness. It is, rather, a life together, a life rooted in the fellowship of God's own life as Father, Son, and Holy Spirit. It is a life in the glad company of fellow sinners, that is a life in the church.

Let us pray: I believe, O Lord, that Jesus is the way, the truth, and the life. Help me to follow him. And when the path grows weary and I feel lonely, give me the gift of your Spirit, the gift of your church, the gift of other saints whose lives strengthen and encourage me in the faith. I pray this in Christ's name. Amen.

Psalm 145

I will extol you, my God and King, and bless your
     name forever and ever.
Every day I will bless you, and praise your name
     forever and ever.
Great is the Lord, and greatly to be praised; his
     greatness is unsearchable.

One generation shall laud your works to another,
     And shall declare your mighty acts.
On the glorious splendor of your majesty,
     And on your wondrous works, I will meditate.
The might of your awesome deeds shall be
     proclaimed,
     And I will declare your greatness.
They shall celebrate the fame of your abundant
     goodness,
     And shall sing aloud of your righteousness.

The Lord is gracious and merciful, slow to anger and
     abounding in steadfast love.
The Lord is good to all, and his compassion is over
     all that he has made.

All your works shall give thanks to you, O Lord,
     And all your faithful shall bless you.
They shall speak of the glory of your kingdom, and
     tell of your power,
     To make known to all people your mighty deeds,
     And the glorious splendor of your kingdom.
Your kingdom is an everlasting kingdom,

*And your dominion endures throughout all
generations.*

*The Lord is faithful in all his words, and gracious in
all his deeds.*
*The Lord upholds all who are falling, and raises up
all who are bowed down.*
*The eyes of all look to you, and you give them their
food in due season.*
*You open your hand, satisfying the desire of every
living thing.*
*The Lord is just in all his ways, and kind in all his
doings.*
*The Lord is near to all who call on him, to all who
call on him in truth.*
*He fulfills the desire of all who fear him; he also
hears their cry, and saves them.*
*The Lord watches over all who love him, but all the
wicked he will destroy.*

*My mouth will speak the praise of the Lord,
And all flesh will bless his holy name forever and
ever.*

DAY 27

— ❦ —

PSALM 145

THE LAST SEVERAL PSALMS IN THE BOOK OF PSALMS ARE SONGS OF PRAISE AND THANKSGIVING. THEY FORM A FINAL CRESCENDO OF PRAISE TO THE GOD OF ISRAEL. Psalm 145 praises God's faithfulness: "The Lord is faithful in all his words, and gracious in all his deeds." That is where our faith comes from, you know. We do not manufacture it or have some special experience that gives us something other folks do not have. Rather, our faith is an echo, a response, an answer to God's prior faithfulness. We risk something as venturesome as faith because God is faithful; his promise is sure. The psalmists love the word "steadfast." God shows up. His love is unremitting. Because he loves us like that, we can risk trying to love one another; we can risk trying to be faithful, too. So do our prayers become an answer to God's word of grace; our eating a thanksgiving (eucharis) for God's prior grace (charis); our lives an offering in response to God's gift of life in Jesus Christ.

"I will extol you, my God and King, and bless your name forever and ever." The psalmist believes that you and I were made for praise. That is not how we view things. We tend to think that we were made to be good tennis players or lawyers or doctors or consumers. But in fact, we are made for much more than that. We are made for singing. Well, you say, "I cannot sing." No matter. You do not have to sing in the choir for your life to sing. Taking delight in God "lifts up one's heart." It is a way of singing.

But what good is singing? What possible use can it be? Not much, really. Worship is always "useless." In fact, when we try to make it "useful," we pervert it. All worship is good for is love. All it is good for is delight. All it is good for is joy. Worship is a kind of wasting of time with God, "hanging out" with him. You cannot make such a gift "pay off." All you can do is enjoy it. You cannot buy it or sell it or make it efficient. You can only receive it as a gift. Yet who wants to live without love, or delight, or joy? Unless we receive such things, we lose heart. We die. We are made for joy, and without the joy of God's love, we wither and perish. So, although we think worship cannot be "used," its praise is, nevertheless, the greatest gift of all.

I remember once reading an interview with a pastor of a "megachurch" who bragged about how many cars could be parked in the church's parking lot and even more, how rapidly the parking lot could be emptied after service. "It's so efficient," he said. But, I thought to myself, worship is not efficient. Praise is not an achievement. Wasting time with God is a gift.

"One generation shall laud your works to another, and shall declare your mighty acts." That also happens in worship. It was the gift my mother gave me in teaching me to pray. It is what parents do for children in lining out the hymns for them in worship. It is what I hope this book of prayers helps to do for you. When one generation seeks to praise God's works to another, it is as if one generation is trying to teach the songs of faith to another, instilling in them the story of God's mighty acts.

"The Lord is gracious and merciful, slow to anger and abounding in steadfast love. The Lord is good to all, and his compassion is over all that he has made." It is not just that

God is Lord or that worship makes some kind of sense. It is that God is good, compassionate, loving. Some people think that the Old Testament is severe, while the New Testament is kind and gentle, but there are simply no more generous words in all the Bible than these: "The Lord is gracious and merciful, slow to anger and abounding in steadfast love." That is gospel. God is good. God, the God of Israel and the church, cares about the least, the little, the dying, the poor, those in college behind in their reading and studying for an exam, as well as those paid to clean up students' rooms, patrol their streets, clean their buildings. "The Lord upholds all who are falling, and raises up all who are bowed down." Is there better news than this? The God who is faithful keeps his eye on the sparrow, cares about those who try and fail, raising up "all who are bowed down."

"The eyes of all look to you, and you give them their food in due season." We are needy folk. There is no shame in admitting that. In fact, we lie when we try to convince ourselves and others that we have no needs, that we are self-sufficient. The truth is that our self-sufficiency is exposed every morning when we wake up and again around noon and again in the evening: We get hungry. We cannot last more than three hours without being reminded of our hunger, our need for food, indeed, our need for God. "The eyes of all look to you."

"You open your hand, satisfying the desire of every living thing." In more ways than we think, believing in God is like eating. We eat so much junk food in our society and it never satisfies. It is only fuel and not very good fuel at that, so that we can be on our way. But God insists we come to a table, that we sit down and break bread with him. In the breaking of the bread and drinking of the wine, and through the opening of Scripture, God converses with us and reveals himself. Eating with God is not fast food. We have to stop and be still for a moment. But this food truly nourishes us.

This food gives us strength to do his will. "You open your hand, satisfying the desire of every living thing."

Let us pray: Open my hands and my heart to receive the good things you give, O Lord. Help me always to hunger for the bread of life, even Jesus Christ. For it is in his name I live and pray. Amen.

Psalm 146

Praise the Lord!
Praise the Lord, O my soul!
I will praise the Lord as long as I live;
*   I will sing praises to my God all my life long.*

Do not put your trust in princes, in mortals, in whom
*   there is no help.*
When their breath departs, they return to the earth;
*   On that very day their plans perish.*

Happy are those whose help is the God of Jacob,
*   Whose hope is in the Lord their God,*
Who made heaven and earth, the sea, and all that is
*   in them;*
Who keeps faith forever; who executes justice for the
*   oppressed;*
*   Who gives food to the hungry.*

The Lord sets the prisoners free; the Lord opens the
*   eyes of the blind.*
The Lord lifts up those who are bowed down; the
*   Lord loves the righteous.*
The Lord watches over the strangers; he upholds the
*   orphan and the widow,*
*   But the way of the wicked he brings to ruin.*

The Lord will reign forever, your God, O Zion, for all
*   generations.*
Praise the Lord!

DAY 28

PSALM 146

THIS TOO IS A PSALM OF PRAISE, A PART OF THE BOOK OF PSALMS' FINAL TRUMPET BLAST OF "HALLELUJAHS." "PRAISE THE LORD! PRAISE THE LORD, O MY SOUL! I WILL praise the Lord as long as I live."

Every emotion seems to be expressed in the book of Psalms: the ups and downs, the moments of joy and despair, the struggle with our own hearts to be faithful, and sometimes even the cursing and anger aimed at our "enemies," even at God. Everything comes out in this book. Therefore, it is doubly significant that the book ends on such a high note of praise. It is almost as if the reader of these psalms has gone through a storm only to emerge finally in the bright light of blue sky and sunshine. Whatever else has happened, whatever failures and sorrows there have been, life before God has this marvelously happy ending, this singing of joy and praise.

"Happy are those whose help is the God of Jacob." Happy are those who follow this God. Put not your trust in celebrities or the culture that thinks it needs celebrities. The glamour, the quick fix, the cheap thrill, these things do not sustain life. Rather, put your hope in the Lord who made heaven and earth. The God of Jacob watched over Jacob when he tried to run away from everybody, including himself, leading Jacob to confess one night at Bethel: "Surely the Lord is in this place—and I did not know it!"

(Gen. 28:16) God is steadfast and true. He finds us even when we think we cannot be found.

Years ago, I pastored a church in which there was a family that was deeply troubled. One evening I got a call from the mother, who told me that her son had run away and had gone with some friends to a lake. Would I go and see about him and try to talk him into coming home? I set out. The lake was a U.S. Army Corps of Engineers lake and was very large. As I drove down the highway, I began to wonder what kind of fool's errand I was on. The lake was so big, its shore so wide. How would I ever find this little boy? I drove off the highway and onto a dirt road that led up to one of the entrances to the lake. When I got there, I turned and drove along the shore until I saw a group of boys building a fire on the beach. There was the son who was missing. I drove up to him, and truly I do not know who was more surprised, he or I. "Get in the car, Billy," I said. "Let's go home." I had found him. With no great skill or preparation or heroic effort, I had found him, or rather, God had led me to him. Billy got in the car, and we took the long road home.

The word "pastor" has something to do with shepherds and sheep. Jesus told many stories of the Good Shepherd who risked all to find his lost sheep. Such stories are what make the otherwise ridiculous job of pastoring possible. The seeker of lost sheep is willing to use anybody, even lost sinners themselves, to help him find his sheep.

This God who "gives food to the hungry" takes a particular interest in those who are lost, in those who have nothing, in those who are belittled and made to feel small, in those who are hungry and wretched. This is one of the ways God sets himself apart from all the other deities that have ever tried to occupy the minds of human beings. The gods we make are interested in the powerful, the wealthy, the famous. The gods we make are often bullies, and we imagine that it would be cool to have such untrammeled power. But the creator of heaven and earth has "his eye on the sparrow"; he notes the hurts of his little ones and refuses to let the powerful run roughshod over the weak.

The Christian faith can be justifiably criticized for many things, but, in truth, the best news any of us ever hears is of the God who takes great interest in "the least of these." That is the true ground of our freedom, the true basis of all justice and equity. If we dismiss this God as unimportant or out of date, we are cutting the ground of freedom out from under our own feet.

The psalmist ends his song of praise by recounting all the ways in which the creator of heaven and earth interests himself in those who are in need. "The Lord sets the prisoners free; the Lord opens the eyes of the blind. The Lord lifts up those who are bowed down; the Lord loves the righteous. The Lord watches over the strangers; he upholds the orphan and the widow, but the way of the wicked he brings to ruin."

This is a wonderful psalm, a psalm of praise to the God who outlasts tyrants and dictators, emperors and kings, only to find his lost sheep through the gift of a little child whose birth pulled shepherds from their fields and wise men from their homes far away, revealing to them all the way home through his own life. That child has given hope to every fatherless and motherless child, to widows and orphans, to the imprisoned and those who are bowed down. He gives hope to you and to me. The night he was born there was singing, too. Indeed, that was what startled the shepherds. No wonder then that the psalmist sings, "Praise the Lord!" No wonder he ends with the best news of all: "The Lord will reign forever, your God, O Zion, for all generations. Praise the Lord!"

Let us pray: Lord, I would sing to you this day, sing a song in my heart and with my voice. I would sing of the good things you have done, the gifts you have given, the love you have poured out on me. Help me to sing like that, to sing and be happy in your service. In Christ's name, I pray. Amen.

NOTES

Psalm 147

Praise the Lord!

How good it is to sing praises to our God;
*   For he is gracious, and a song of praise is fitting.*
The Lord builds up Jerusalem; he gathers the outcasts
*   of Israel.*
He heals the brokenhearted, and binds up their
*   wounds.*
He determines the number of the stars; he gives to all
*   of them their names.*
Great is our Lord, and abundant in power; his
*   understanding is beyond measure.*
The Lord lifts up the downtrodden; he casts the
*   wicked to the ground.*

Sing to the Lord with thanksgiving; make melody to
*   our God on the lyre.*
He covers the heavens with clouds, prepares rain for
*   the earth,*
*   Makes grass grow on the hills.*
He gives to the animals their food, and to the young
*   ravens when they cry.*
His delight is not in the strength of the horse,
*   Nor his pleasure in the speed of a runner;*
*   But the Lord takes pleasure in those who fear*
*   him,*
*   In those who hope in his steadfast love.*
Praise the Lord, O Jerusalem! Praise your God, O
*   Zion!*
For he strengthens the bars of your gates; he blesses
*   your children within you.*

*He grants peace within your borders; he fills you
 with the finest of wheat.
He sends out his command to the earth; his word
 runs swiftly.
He gives snow like wool; he scatters frost like ashes.
He hurls down hail like crumbs—who can stand
 before his cold?
He sends out his word and melts them;
 He makes his wind blow, and the waters flow.
He declares his word to Jacob, his statutes and
 ordinances to Israel.
He has not dealt thus with any other nation; they do
 not know his ordinances.
Praise the Lord!*

DAY 29

——◆——

PSALM 147

"HOW GOOD IT IS TO SING PRAISES TO OUR GOD; FOR HE IS GRACIOUS, AND A SONG OF PRAISE IS FITTING." "FITTING," APPROPRIATE, JUST RIGHT, THESE ARE SOME OF THE WAYS the psalmist thinks that praising God makes life beautiful. At times I am overwhelmed with the beauty of worship, when the Christian faith in its praise of God seems to me to be simply beautiful. I know we do not think that way very often. More often, we think of the faith as something difficult or perhaps as a duty we must perform. Occasionally, we see good people of faith who inspire us and impress us with their acts of sacrifice or costly witness. But I wonder whether we are not just as moved, if not more, by the beauty of faith's imagination.

A few years ago, my wife and I celebrated our twenty-fifth anniversary by going to Europe. One day we found ourselves in the lovely town of Chartres in France, and we spent the afternoon walking through the magnificent cathedral there. Rarely have I been so moved. The darkness on the inside combined with the brilliant light streaming through the stained glass windows to make me feel as if I were at the gates of heaven. It was all so beautiful. Faith had made this beautiful place, bringing the worshiper to adoration and praise.

Perhaps you have had a similar experience. On Easter our congregation sings Handel's "Hallelujah Chorus," during which the claims of the Christian faith are affirmed in all their robust particularity, happily and unapologetically celebrated before the world. This must be what heaven sounds like, I think.

But the imagination of faith is not confined to worship's sights and sounds. Occasionally, one encounters a life that is not just good or dutifully pious but is, simply, beautiful. Such a life has far more influence, I suspect, than an instructive "good example." Such a life, rather, attracts and inspires. Such a life is "fitting" in that it corresponds with its own beauty to the glory of God's self-giving.

The glory of God that the psalmist celebrates as something beautiful is not quite the same thing that we might define as beautiful. It is God's generosity to the poor, his love of the small and overlooked, that defines his beauty. "He gathers the outcasts of Israel." "He heals the brokenhearted and binds up their wounds." "The Lord lifts up the downtrodden." His delight is not in "horsepower" or in the "speed of a runner," "but the Lord takes pleasure in those who fear him, in those who hope in his steadfast love."

He takes pleasure, delight, a sense of beauty in those who risk believing in his steadfast love. Do you know what it is to be a beautiful person? A really beautiful person? It is to sing this psalm, to pray it, and to let it fill your life. Following Jesus Christ does not win you any beauty contests, but it involves you in a life of generosity and joy, a life that radiates beauty and grace from the inside out. When Malcolm Muggeridge wrote his biography of Mother Teresa, he entitled it *Something Beautiful for God.* Mother Teresa was beautiful in this truest sense. She was "beautiful for God." That is the gift of the Christian life, not to become like Mother Teresa but to become God's beautiful children, to glorify him with our lives, to enjoy him, "fittingly," reflecting his glory in our service. As George Bailey learned, such a life is indeed, "a wonderful life." It may take an angel to help us see it (it nearly always has, by the way) or a psalm to help us sing it, but it is a wonderful life.

Let us pray: Father, I thank you for the beauty of each day: for sunshine and shadow, for morning and evening, for sounds and sights that make me glad to be alive. Give me grace to live for you, to lose myself in the happy praise of your goodness and grace. I thank you that you are not the God who delights in sheer power or who is swayed by the famous or who is enthralled by the amassing of wealth, but that you seem much more interested in those who have little or nothing, those who suffer, those whom we so easily forget. Give to me your Holy Spirit that I might see what you would have me see and find in the least of these, not just my brothers and sisters, but even more, your beautiful children. In the name of Jesus Christ the Lord, I pray. Amen.

NOTES

Psalm 150

Praise the Lord!
Praise God in his sanctuary; praise him in his mighty
    firmament!
Praise him for his mighty deeds;
Praise him according to his surpassing greatness!

Praise him with trumpet sound;
Praise him with lute and harp!
Praise him with tambourine and dance;
Praise him with strings and pipe!
Praise him with clanging cymbals;
Praise him with loud clashing cymbals!
Let everything that breathes praise the Lord!
Praise the Lord!

DAY 30

PSALM 150

THE BOOK OF PSALMS ENDS WITH THIS FINAL "HALLELUJAH!" THAT INVITES "EVERYTHING THAT BREATHES" TO PRAISE THE LORD. IT IS NOTHING MORE than an exhortation to all creation to join with Israel in this final song of praise.

"Praise God in his sanctuary." This is the place where the praise of God begins, where the otherwise silent praise of all creation comes to voice and song, making those of us who worship the "pipes" through which creation itself, like some mighty organ, erupts in praise. "Praise him for his mighty deeds; praise him according to his surpassing greatness!" The praise of God requires memory. "Once we were slaves in Egypt," Israel remembered, "and the Lord delivered us with a mighty hand." Memory of God's "mighty deeds"—the crossing of the Red Sea, manna in the wilderness, the toppling of the walls of Jericho, deliverance again and again—this was the stuff of Israel's memory and faith. "If it had not been the Lord who was on our side—let Israel now say—if it had not been the Lord who was on our side, when our enemies attacked us, then they would have swallowed us up alive." (Ps. 124) Recalling God's "mighty deeds" was the way Israel confessed her faith, the way she "praised the Lord." This is not merely an interesting historical lesson, but is, in fact, the way we too confess our faith. God's mightiest deed, we believe, was raising Jesus Christ from the dead. That is why we gather for worship: to tell and retell that deed; to remember it, and to hope in its promise for the whole world. Praise the Lord!

Then the psalmist goes a little bit crazy. He wants music, and not only quiet chamber music or lush violins. He wants ear-splitting, dance-making, celebration-happening music to praise the Lord. "Praise him with trumpet sound; praise him with lute and harp! Praise him with tambourine and dance; praise him with strings and pipe! Praise him with clanging cymbals; praise him with loud clashing cymbals!" Sometimes the praise of God must be unrestrained, a joyful letting go of our hearts in utter happiness and praise. Sometimes it helps to be a little crazy in worshiping this God.

I can remember when my wife said "Yes" to my proposal of marriage and how giddily happy I was. I remember when each of our children was born. I was so happy that I went a little crazy. I remember moments in my life when words were not enough, when I was so happy that I felt that I was about to jump out of my own skin. When we feel that way, we come close to what this psalmist is feeling in this last triumphant blast of praise.

The psalm concludes with the words: "Let everything that breathes praise the Lord! Praise the Lord!"

That is how I would like this book of meditations and prayers to end, and more important, how I would like my life and yours to end: as a final, happy doxology. In the end, that is all that we have to offer God: our thanks and praise. To learn what the birds of the air and the lilies of the field know already is the great gift and calling of the Christian life: to praise God with our very being. Nothing more. We go to worship to learn our lines, to catch the tune, to sing the music that praises God for all his goodness. It may be an extravagant hope, but I do hope that this book helps lead you into such a life and into such happy songs. The book of Psalms, like the Bible itself, has a happy ending. It ends with praise. So may our lives end in the singing of such happy songs of praise. "Let everything that breathes praise the Lord! Praise the Lord!"

Let us pray: Our Father, teach me the music, give me the song, grant me the heart to sing your praises every day. Just so, I would be like a bird of the air or a lily of the field and praise you with my life. Make me a living part of that worshiping community without whose help I will never be able to sing and without whose hope I will never be able to know you aright. With them, I would remember your mighty acts, the surpassing beauty of your steadfast love, the hope of a world redeemed in Jesus Christ. In his life grant me that freedom to serve you all my days, loving the world you have made and declared good, a world that is yet in need of hearing the happy songs of your praise and love. I ask you this in the name of your mightiest deed, even Jesus Christ your Son, in whose name I pray. Amen.

NOTES

NOTES